PSYCHE AND BIBLE

three old testament themes

RIVKAH SCHÄRF KLUGER

1974

SPRING PUBLICATIONS

c/o Postfach 190
8024 Zürich
Switzerland

Spring Publications, The Analytical Psychology Club of New York, Inc.
Suite 306, 130 East 39th Street, New York City 10016

ISBN 0-88214-107-4

Composed, Photo-offset and Manufactured in Switzerland
by Buchdruckerei Schrumpf, 8123 Ebmatingen Zürich
for Spring Publications, Postfach 190, 8024 Zürich

Cover by: Jan Luss

CONTENTS

THE IDEA OF THE CHOSEN PEOPLE

PREFATORY NOTE

THE IDEA OF THE CHOSEN PEOPLE

"The Idea of the Chosen People: A Contribution to the Symbolism of Individuation" was given first as a seminar at the C. G. Jung Institute Zürich, Summer Semester 1953. The material was presented again at the Psychological Club Zürich in February 1955, and subsequently to the Analytical Psychology Club of Los Angeles.

The translation was made by Murray Stein and then revised into the present version by the author.

I

The concept of the chosen people has become suspect in our day. Appearing to live on only as an "enlightened" misunderstanding, or inflated abuse, something embarrassing is attached to it. It had already become merely an embarrassment early in Reform Judaism. Abraham Geiger (1810-1875), a leader of German Reform Judaism, struck from the passages in the prayerbooks that mention the election of Israel the words "from among all the peoples,"[1] and his footsteps are followed by many American Reform Rabbis today.[2] These efforts may have sprung from the sympathetic trait of human modesty, but perhaps they also express a state of "weariness with being chosen" which is rooted in the unconscious depths of the Jewish people as a whole. Weighed down by the curse of being chosen, they long for nothing more than normality, for "being like all the people," which is more than understandable. It is certain, however, that merely brushing aside or repudiating this idea, which seemingly has become incomprehensible and unacceptable, would amount to a "loss of soul," since it is the central idea of the Old Testament.

If one accepts the idea that the Bible is the written record of profound religious experiences, and in this sense "inspired," one must also take seriously the idea of the chosen people, for it belongs to the main stock of fundamental religious experiences in the Old Testament. The danger of this idea, its "shadow" so to speak, is hubris, i.e., the danger that the ego of the people, carried by the individuals who are identified with it, may take possession in an inflationary way of this content that originates in the Self, or may be overwhelmed by it. This danger is great and was all the greater the more primitive the time, i.e., the closer to the constellation of a primitive society where the individual still lived to a great extent in *participation mystique* with the group.

We shall see that the prophets were confronted with this danger and in the name of God emphatically strove to make their contemporaries

3

conscious of it. But also in our time, equipped as it is with a greater possibility of consciousness, one cannot escape this danger by withdrawing from a confrontation with it. On the contrary, unconsciously one can become its victim all the more, as is the case with all repressed psychic contents. Perhaps the time has come to look objectively, *sine ira et studio,* into what the Old Testament says about the chosen people and what significance is given to this idea in the sphere of Old Testament religion.

Perhaps a new, *psychological* understanding of this burdensome idea will emerge which may give it again, on an inner level, its inherent dignity. For we may not simply strip off something that belongs to our inner history without suffering damage to the soul. We must try to grasp the *symbolic content* of such statements; it then remains open whether they become renovated building blocks of the inner life or prove themselves truly worn out. That the danger of hubris is not unavoidable is shown by the fact that there were great individuals who did understand it; the prophets, old Talmudic teachers, Chassidic Zaddikim. Of them we shall have more to say later.

Uneasiness with the idea of Israel's being the chosen people is not restricted to Jewish circles, be it because the daughters of Judaism, Christianity and Islam, also consider themselves "chosen," [3] as Lessing stresses in *Nathan der Weise,* or because Jewish "chosenness" stands irritatingly and disturbingly in the way of the understanding of many Christian theologians. Robert Smend, for example, speaks of the belief of the Jews in being chosen as an "offensive claim" to other peoples, [4] a viewpoint that G. Quell, [5] on the other hand, reproaches as lacking comprehension vis-á-vis the idea of the chosen people. At any rate, a *malaise* is mirrored in this theological controversy, which may be the reason why the idea of the chosen people has scarcely found monographic treatment.

This is pointed out by H.H. Rowley, one of the few authors who has dealt with the problem of the chosen people. He goes on, however, to prove himself involuntarily affected by the same uneasiness when he remarks: "Whether we like it or not, the doctrine of election is a Biblical doctrine, and whatever our view of its validity, it demands some attention from the student of the Bible."[6]   3(5)-1-1+

The work of a Dutch Protestant theologian, Th. Vriezen,[7] provides a good survey of the treatment of this problem on the Jewish and Christian sides. But after a good initial presentation of the problem Vriezen does not venture beyond the views of the other works, which are characterized by the theological barrier.

This study is an attempt to understand psychologically the phenomenon of the Old Testament idea of the chosen people. But I cannot hope to consider this phenomenon in all its aspects, for that would broaden it into an encompassing theology of the Old Testament. To start with, the complex problem of the *Brith,* the covenant, will not be examined here. The covenant is a consequence of the election. Likewise it is unnecessary to give a great deal of space to the historical and text-critical problems, since these are for our purposes sufficiently dealt with in an excellent study by Kurt Galling.[8]   He establishes two streams of election tradition: the Exodus (Sinai) tradition and the tradition of the patriarchs, of which the first is the older. This conclusion suggests itself also from the viewpoint of inner psychological development, as will be shown later.

Galling limits himself, however, to tracing the political consequences of this idea in the Old Testament. Consequently, he is unable to advance our understanding of the religious problem of chosenness. This latter aspect is emphasized in the works of H.H. Rowley,[9] G. Quell,[10] and Jizchak Heinemann.[11]   Rowley and Heinemann come to the conclusion that the choice is essentially bound to a purpose, so that the election means primarily not preference but task. They overlook thereby the fact that the character of purposefulness, which in itself is rational, just does not correspond to the situation of the divine choice.

5

Quell, in his differentiated analysis of the concept, manages to avoid this error by taking into consideration also the *irrational aspect* of the divine choice. He illuminates this aspect by throwing light on synonyms and parallel concepts. But for him, too, the exciting question of what may have *caused God* at all to choose a people as *his people* goes begging. One is left only with an allusion to the mystery of divine love.

Thus Quell writes of the divine choice as an "inexplicable fact": "It is explicable and interpretable only in its content, not in the motives..." [12] He then comes to the central point of his exposition: "What remains alive in the Old Testament concept of the chosen people is only the mystery, the inexplicable, which in Deuteronomy is expressed by the words: He loved you." [13] Heinemann mentions that Maimonides also absolutely put aside the question of why God gave his Torah to one particular people, for in his view one can only answer with: "This is how his wisdom wanted it, or how it decided it" *(Moreh Nebuchim 2:25)*.

Rowley, too, puts forward God's wisdom and grace as the final answer and simply declines further consideration of the reason for the divine choice. [14] But with the allusion to the mystery, the inexplicable in the fundamental motive of the divine choice, its irrationality is implicitly acknowledged; the question of this basic motive becomes thereby a *psychological* question, referring back to the divine *psyche* of the Old Testament God who reveals himself as a quasi-personal entity. In this audience, reference to the divine psyche and the fact that God appears as quasi-personal will not be misunderstood in the sense of a mere projection of human categories on the Godhead, i.e., an anthropomorphism. I would, however, like to call attention to a highly significant passage in *Symbols of Transformation,* where Jung states:

> There are no conclusive arguments against the hypothesis that these archetypal figures are endowed with personality at the outset and are not just secondary personalizations. In

so far as the archetypes do not represent mere functional relationships, they manifest themselves as *daimones,* as personal agencies. In this form they are felt as actual experiences and are not "figments of the imagination," as rationalism would have us believe. Consequently, man derives his human personality only secondarily from what the myths call his descent from the gods and heroes; or, to put it in psychological terms, *his consciousness of himself as a personality derives primarily from the influence of quasi-personal archetypes.*

> (C.W. 5, para. 388,
> italics mine)

This quality of personality is especially characteristic of the Old Testament God Yahweh, owing to his inner tension of opposites, which led subsequently to transformation and development. In his *Answer to Job,* Jung differentiates the distinct personality of Yahweh, with its intensely personal claim on mankind, from

Father Zeus, who in a benevolent and somewhat detached manner allowed the economy of the universe to roll along its accustomed courses and punished only those who were disorderly. He did not moralize but ruled purely instinctively. He did not demand anything more *from* human beings than the sacrifice due to him; he did not want to do anything *with* human beings because he had no plans for them. *Father Zeus is certainly a figure but not a personality.* Yahweh, on the other hand, was interested in man. Human beings were a matter of first-rate importance to him. He needed them as they needed him, urgently and personally.

> (C.W. 11, para. 568,
> italics mine)

Yahweh's distinct quality of personality is essentially, indeed causally,

7

related to the idea of the chosen people, as will become clear later.

Returning to the theological discussion about God's motive for the election: that the assumption of God's love as the ultimate reason for the election draws attention to the divine psyche and makes the election a psychological question has been correctly understood by G. Quell. He says that the idea of the chosen people is "an objective statement about an event in the *psyche of God,* which is fully graspable in its factual effect" (italics mine). To be sure, he adds immediately the qualification that this "objective statement" is probably beyond the range of human understanding.[15] He goes on: "Because the event of the election is concentrated wholly in the person, even in the feeling, of God, it has a full share in the riddle of all personal feeling."[16] Here he clearly hands the question over to the psychologist, who precisely may not halt before the "riddle of all personal feeling." Precisely at this is his interest aimed. Once the question is put psychologically in this sense, we will find that the texts certainly answer it. In the following, therefore, we will go carefully into the Old Testament passages which deal with the election. Their answer to this question may contain a clue about destiny, not only past but future, and not only Jewish but generally human.

To begin with, it is necessary to examine closely the terms of choosing, and to ask: What kind of expressive power do the words have which designate the choosing act of God? What conclusions do these words allow about the character of the divine subject who carries out the act of choosing?

We are immediately confronted by a highly significant fact: the main verb of choosing, *bāḥar,* in ninety-two of the one hundred and sixty-four passages in which it appears at all in the Old Testament, has *God* for its subject, to which are to be added another thirteen instances of the passive *bāḥir* = "chosen"(by God);[17] this amounts to approximately two-thirds of all the passages in which *bāḥar* occurs. This in itself reveals the predominately *religious* character of the concept of choosing in the Old Testament and, as we shall see, this concept is broader than its *profane* aspect. We must first, however, determine the latter, in order to obtain the full tonal range of the concept in the divine realm.

Bāḥar means "choose," "select," "elect," "prefer." A few examples will be sufficient. In II Samuel 17:1 Ahithophel says to Absalom: "Let me choose twelve thousand men..." Here, as also in II Samuel 10:9 where it is said of Joab that "he chose some of the picked men of Israel, and arrayed them against the Syrians," the act of choosing means in the first place discrimination among different objects, and second, positive decision for one specific object that has an advantage over others. A special *quality* of the thing chosen determines the choice. In the examples it is the fitness of the men for battle, the others being simultaneously eliminated as unfit and rejected. Other passages also, which have to do not with people but objects, show that, originally, a quality of the object determines the choice. Thus the idol-carver in Isaiah 40:20 chooses "wood that will not rot"; Lot "chose" for himself all the Jordan Valley (Gen. 13:11) because he "saw that the Jordan valley was well watered everywhere" (Gen. 13:10).

One can agree with Heinemann [18] that the word in its original meaning refers to a *choice among different things for a specific use.* Thus the *preference* of one thing over another is inherent in the concept of choice. Because of its purpose, however, the preference remains rationally comprehensible. But if the element of purpose falls away, then even in the profane aspect of choosing — profane in the sense of *human* choosing in contradistinction to divine choosing — an emotional element comes to the fore, as in Isaiah 1:15 where it is said of Immanuel:

> He shall eat curds and honey until* he
> knows how to refuse [mā'as] the evil
> and choose [bāḥar] the good.

>   (*Following the translation of the Zürich Bible)

9

Here the immediate purpose of the choice is no longer evident; rather *the capacity to decide, per se,* stands in the foreground. The moral quality of refusing the evil and choosing the good in itself indicates an emotional component. This point becomes more evident where "choose" is contrasted with "hate," as in Proverbs 1:29:

> Because they hated knowledge
> and did not choose the fear of the Lord...

The Zürich Bible translates this passage accordingly:

> ...an der Furcht des Herrn keinen Gefallen hatten...
> ("...did not like the fear of the Lord...")

The emotional character of choosing becomes transparently clear in passages where it stands in closest parallel to verbs expressing *wanting* or *desiring,* as in I Samuel 12:13:

> And now behold the king whom you have *chosen (bāḥar),* for whom you have *asked (šā'al).*
>
> (Italics mine)

Here we meet a parallelism that, as we shall see, also appears on the plane of divine choosing and there takes on decisive significance.

In Isaiah 66:3-4 *bāḥar* appears in parallel to *ḥāfēṣ* ("desire," "take pleasure in"):

> These have *chosen (bāḥarū)* their own ways,
> and their soul *delights in (ḥāfēṣā)*
> their abominations;
> I also will choose affliction for them
> and bring their fears upon them;

because, when I called, no one answered,
when I spoke they did not listen;
but they did what was evil in my eyes,
and *chose (bāharū)* that in which *I
did not delight (lō hāfastī).*

(Italics mine)

The Zürich Bible, in accordance with the parallelism in the text, translates *bāhar* as "Freude haben," "to take joy in":

Wie diese Freude haben *(bāharū)* an ihren Wegen
und ihr Herz sich an den Greueln ergötzt *(hāfēṣā)*...
("As these take joy in *(bāharū)* their ways
and their soul delights in *(hāfēṣā)* their abominations...")

In I Samuel 20:30 Saul says to his son Jonathan:

You son of a perverse, rebellious woman, do I
not know that you have *chosen (bōhēr)* the son of
Jesse to your own shame...?

(Italics mine)

Here the word *bāhar* has the sense of desiring: in Jonathan's "choice" of David as a friend, the factor of *decision* (to be his faithful friend) is linked in the concept of "choice" with the irrational element of feeling himself drawn to him. The Zürich Bible does not hesitate to translate *bāhar* in this sense:

Du Sohn einer Zuchtvergessenen! Ich weiß ja wohl,
daß du an dem Sohne Isais *hängst (bōhēr)*
("...I know well enough that you *cling (bōhēr)*
to the son of Jesse.")

(Italics mine)

11

One must agree with Quell's conclusion about the profane usage of *bāḥar:* "The accents can lie on widely differing points. Choosing can, but need not, proceed from an outspoken rational judgment, but under certain circumstances it is also based on a *feeling or even a compulsion"[19]* (italics mine).

Turning now to the *divine* sphere, we see that the irrational character of choosing moves fully into the foreground in God's choice of the people of Israel. A special qualification of this people is not only not given as the reason for the choice, but is even denied, and this in the key passage of the Old Testament's revelation of the election:

> For you are a *people holy ('am qādōš)* to the Lord your God;
> the Lord your God has *chosen (bāḥar)* you to be a people
> *for his own possession (le'am segullā),* out of all the peoples
> that are on the face of the earth. It was not because you
> were more in number than any other people that the Lord
> *set his love upon you* [ḥāšaq, literally: "to cling to someone]
> and chose you, for you were the fewest of all peoples; but
> it is because the Lord *loves you ('ahabā)* and is keeping the
> oath which he swore to your fathers, that the Lord has
> brought you out with a mighty hand, and redeemed you
> from the house of bondage, from the hand of Pharaoh king
> of Egypt.

(Deut. 7:6-8, italics mine)

This passage contains in itself almost all the essential elements of the phenomenon of election and will occupy us further in the course of our investigation, particularly in connection with the *exodus from Egypt,* a motif that is essentially bound up with the election. I would like first, however, to limit myself to the meaning of the verbs of choice which occur here and in other passages, in order to come to a clearer under- standing of the motif of election through the terminology of choosing; afterwards we will take up *the purpose and consequence of the choice* for both subject and object.

In this passage from Deuteronomy the verb *ḥāšaq* appears in close parallel to *bāḥar*. *Ḥāšaq* is a verb of strongest emotional intensity; it is translated "to set one's love upon," but literally it means "to cling to someone." The reason for Yahweh's choice of Israel is given in this verb: he chose Israel *because he clung to it.* This reason is immediately strengthened by another: "because Yahweh loves you." Thus the text gives the love *('ahabā)* of Yahweh as *the only, irrational reason for the choice,* a reason we find also in reference to Mount Zion:

> He *rejected* the tent of Joseph,
>   he did not choose the tribe of Ephraim;
> but he chose the tribe of Judah,
>   Mount Zion, which he *loves.*

(Psalm 78:67-68, italics mine)

At first sight such passages seem to support the view that this love of God is the ultimate reason for the election, beyond which one cannot and may not penetrate any further. The verbs of choosing, however, throw some additional light on the nature of this love and allow us to see more deeply into the divine psychic process. This love of God is not a totally "selfless," undemanding love; there is desire in it and need for the other, an irrational passion to have the other for oneself. This point becomes even more evident when we consider the purpose of the election and its consequences for subject and object as these are expressed in this passage from Deuteronomy.

Yahweh chooses Israel from among all the peoples *for himself, to make it the people of his own possession ('am segullā). Segullā* means possession. The Babylonian *sugullu* originally relates to herds, the valuable property of farmers. It means the belonging of a property to its owner. In Ecclesiastes 2:8 *segullā* is the king's treasure, and in I Chronicles 29:3

David speaks of his treasure of gold and silver as his *segullā*. In Psalm
135:4 *segullā* is God's possession and occurs in connection with *bāḥar:*

> For the Lord has chosen Jacob for himself,
> Israel as his own possession.

Another term which designates the people as God's possession is
naḥalā. *Naḥalā* also means possession, but especially ownership of land
that has come into one's possession through inheritance. Here the
emphasis lies on the fatefulness of the property falling into one's possession. The designation of Israel as God's *inheritance* is really very
remarkable. One might ask: from whom did he inherit it? Presumably
from an earlier owner, whose heir he was. Several passages in Deuteronomy where *naḥalā* is used to designate the people of God and is linked
with the exodus from Egypt (Deut. 4:20; 9:26, 29) suggest that it was
Egypt, which in the Old Testament has a mother-connotation, from whom
Yahweh received his inheritance. It is from Egypt that he redeems his
people and *chooses* it as his inheritance.

Just as fateful, and perhaps even more emphasized, is another term
for the divine possession, namely *ḥeleq*, "portion," "share," which has
in the Old Testament, however, the actual meaning of "lot," "fate."
The word occurs in Isaiah 17:14 parallel with *gōrāl*, the fated course of
the stars. Deuteronomy 32:9 links *naḥalā*, "inheritance," and *ḥeleq*,
"portion," with a third word, *ḥebel*, "the allotted," "the apportioned:"

> For the Lord's portion *(ḥeleq)* is his people,
> Jacob his alloted heritage *(ḥebel naḥalatō)*.

It continues in a way that is significant for our whole context:

> He found him in a desert land,
> and in the howling waste of the wilderness;

> he encircled him, he cared for him,
> he kept him as the apple of his eye.

> (Deut. 32:10)

In Zachariah 2:12 (2:16 in the Hebrew text) the concepts *nāḥal* and *ḥeleq* are coupled with *bāḥar:*

> And the Lord will inherit *(nāḥal)* Judah as his
> portion *(ḥelqō)* in the holy land, and will again
> choose *(bāḥar)* Jerusalem.

Especially revealing, it seems to me, is a passage in Jeremiah where not only is Israel called the portion of Yahweh, but Yahweh is also called the portion *(ḥeleq)* of Jacob *(ḥeleq Ya 'aqōb)*, i.e., of Israel:

> Not like these [i.e., the idols] is he
> who is the portion of Jacob *(ḥeleq Ya 'aqōb)*,
> for he is the one who formed all things,
> and Israel is the tribe of his inheritance *(naḥalatō)*.

> (Jer. 10:16)

Here the idea that God, too, has a fate is implied. In a relationship, both sides are embraced by fate: if one is the fate of the other, the reverse also holds true. The imperative necessity that man *consciously chooses* this fate of being God's inheritance receives impressive expression in Joshua 24, where Joshua at the assembly in Shechem says:

> Now therefore fear the Lord, and serve him
> in sincerity and faithfulness; put away the
> gods which your fathers served beyond the
> River, and in Egypt, and serve the Lord.
> And if you be unwilling to serve the Lord,
> choose this day whom you will serve, whether

15

> the gods your fathers served in the region
> beyond the River, or the gods of the Amorites
> in whose land you dwell; but as for me and
> my house, we will serve the Lord.
>
> (Joshua 24:14-15)

And as the people, mindful of their redemption from Egypt, decide for Yahweh, Joshua says to them:

> You are witnesses *against yourselves* that
> you have chosen the Lord, to serve him.
> And they said: "We are witnesses."
>
> (Joshua 24:22, italics mine)

On the human side, the acceptance of the election, the moral decision, stands in the foreground, but also included is the act of becoming conscious of the regressive tendency which resists the election; this latter factor, to my mind, makes this passage extraordinarily significant from a psychological point of view.

Let us return to the problem of the motivation behind God's choice. We saw that Yahweh chooses Israel from among all the peoples *for himself*, in order to make it his *possession*. But why does he want a people for himself, a people to belong to him as his own? Indirectly Deuteronomy 7:6ff. itself provides an answer to this question: he chooses it for his own possession so that it shall be a holy people *('am qādōš)*. A "people of his own" and a "holy people" are, so to speak, synonymous:

> For you are a people holy *('am qādōš)* to
> the Lord your God; the Lord your God has
> chosen you to be a people for his own possession
> *('am segullā),* out of all the peoples that
> are on the face of the earth.
>
> (Deut. 7:6)

16

In Numbers 16:5, *belonging to God, holiness,* and *being chosen* appear
as identical states of being. Moses says to Korah:

> In the morning the Lord will show *who is*
> *his,* and *who is holy,* and will cause him
> to come near to him; him *whom he will choose*
> he will cause to come near to him.

> (Italics mine)

The oracular mysteriousness of the act of election comes beautifully
to the fore in this passage, and this underscores and heightens its irrational, numinous quality.

Thus Israel is to be a holy people, an *'am qādōš*. Now *qādōš* in its
original sense means "singled out." Being singled out, which belongs by
definition to the concept of election, is here explicitly mentioned as
the *purpose* of the election: *it becomes a value in itself.* In Deuteronomy
28:9 the election of this people as a holy people is, however, linked to
a condition:

> The Lord will establish you as a people holy
> to himself, as he has sworn to you, *if* you
> keep the commandments of the Lord your God,
> and walk in his ways.

> (Italics mine)

And in Exodus 19:6 the claim becomes even more clear:

> ...and you shall be to me a kingdom
> of priests and a holy nation.

Thus the purpose of this sanctification is that the people consecrate itself
to God. In the Old Testament, living according to the Law means sancti-

17

fying life. One must live according to a law other than only the law of nature. As I have stated in another context,[20] the meaning of the Law seems to me to lie in the fact that it lifts man out of the conflict-free state of animal nature. He is placed in the situation of conflict, which is the precondition for becoming conscious. Deuteronomy 30:11-14 shows, moreover, that in the Old Testament itself there already exists an inwardly oriented conception of the Law:

> For this commandment which I command you
> this day is not too hard for you, neither
> is it far off. It is not in heaven, that you
> should say, "who will go up for us to
> heaven, and bring it to us, that we may hear
> it and do it? " Neither is it beyond the
> sea, that you should say, "who will go
> over the sea for us, and bring it to us,
> that we may hear it and do it? " But the
> word is very near you; it is in your mouth
> and in your heart, so that you can do it.

We still, however, need to tackle the question, what is Yahweh's motive for making Israel into a holy people, for imposing the Law on it? Why should it be singled out, made holy? We find the answer in Leviticus 21:8:

> ...for I the Lord, who sanctify you,
> am holy.

The same is stated especially clearly in Leviticus 20:26; there it is linked with another verb of distinguishing and singling out, *hibdîl:*

> You shall be holy to me; for *I the Lord*
> *am holy,* and have separated *('abdîl)* you
> from the peoples, that you should be mine.
>
> (Italics mine)

18

Because Yahweh is himself holy, his people should be holy, belonging to him, so to speak, as his counterpart. Although "holy" *(qādōš)* has here, in the self-designation of Yahweh, a fuller tone, embracing the aspects of purity and numinosity, it may, on the basis of the direct parallelism between "holy" and "separated from," be understood also in its original meaning of "being singled out." If this people is singled out from all the peoples, *Yahweh must also be singled out from among all the gods.*

The Godhead Yahweh, who has, so to speak, grown together from many polytheistic god-figures into a God-personality, has become thereby a *distinct* God, who stands out from all the other gods. This distinct God now chooses for himself an equally distinct people as his vis-á-vis. Here we see, projected onto a people, the birth of the idea of the *individual* who is removed from the anonymous existence in the cycle of nature and placed into a personal, unique fate.

What we meet here is a collective individual, as evidenced in Deuteronomy, the main source of the election idea, where the people is addressed predominantly in the second person singular. Often also the patriarchs stand for the whole people. To a certain extent, the tradition of the election of the patriarchs represents a further development, that is, the transition *from the purely collective image of the people to an individual who represents it.* That the patriarchs stand unambiguously for the people is shown, for example, in Psalm 135:4:

> For the Lord has chosen Jacob for himself,
> Israel as his own possession.

and still more markedly in Isaiah 41:8-10:

> But you, Israel, my *servant,*
> Jacob, whom I have *chosen,*

the offspring of Abraham, my friend [*ōhabī*, literally
"beloved"];
you whom I took [*heḥezīq*, literally "grasped"] from the
ends of the earth,
and called *(qārā')* from its farthest corners,
saying to you, "You are my servant,
I have *chosen* you and not *cast you off*";
fear not, for I am with you...

(Italics mine)

This passage contains two further parallel terms for the election, *heḥezīq* or "to fetch," "grasp," "seize," and *qārā'*, "to call." Both strengthen the idea of God's choice as a *claim*. God fetches, calls, desires; hence, he needs. He needs the singled-out people. In God's loving choice his need is revealed. But what kind of need is this? What is it that God needs? Here another word, used as a synonym for the verb *bāḥar*, points the way to a solution: *yāda'*. *Yāda'*, a verb whose meaning is most complex, replaces *bāḥar* in several significant passages. It means "to perceive," "to become conscious of," "to experience," "to recognize," "to know." Denoting an active acquisition of knowledge, it might be best rendered by "to know through experience." Its range of meaning in the Old Testament extends from sexual union [Gen. 4:1, 17, 25 (Eve); Gen. 19:8 (Lot's daughters); Gen. 24:16 (Rebekah); Gen. 38:26 (Tamar); Judges 11:39 (Jephthah's daughter)] to the most subtle act of knowing, as in Deuteronomy 34:10, where it is said of Moses that "the Lord *knew* [him] face to face." "To conceive," "grasp," "become aware of" contain both meanings, the spiritual component of the sexual act and the love aspect in the spiritual act of knowing.

Quell thinks that the sexual meaning of *yāda'* is merely a euphemistic usage. The connection of meaning between love and knowledge described above speaks against this notion. It is also not evident why the euphemistic substitute should be precisely *yāda'*. [21]

20

Now, the verb *yāda'* is used in place of *bāḥar* in several very significant passages of the Old Testament, as for instance in Hosea 13:5:

> It was I who knew you *(yeda'tīkā)* in the wilderness,
>> in the land of drought

That one may here justifiably translate *yāda'* ("know") with "choose," as the Zürich Bible actually does, is supported by several similar passages, especially Jeremiah 1:5:

> Before I formed you in the womb I *knew* you,
>> and before you were born I *consecrated* you
>>> [*hiqdaštīkā* or made holy, singled out];
> I *appointed* you a prophet to the nations.

> > > > > (Italics mine)

We have here a very good Old Testament example of the feeling of fate, connected with an individual's experience of being chosen. Here also, being chosen means being sanctified, singled out, for the service of God. We shall see later on that the idea of chosenness finds its fullest expression in the "servant of God," who appears in Isaiah's so-called "Songs of the Servant of God" (Chap. 40ff).

Thus, in the verb *yāda'* we find, over and above the loving search for the other, *the aspect of knowing.* In being found, the essence of the other person is revealed, and with that he steps into responsibility; he can no longer escape. *He is found.* This profound inner relation becomes evident in the significant passage, Amos 3:2:

> You only have I known *(yāda')*
>> of all the families of the earth;
> *therefore I will punish you*
>> *for all your iniquities.*

> > > > > (Italics mine)

21

Here, being distinct becomes being meant. For the "called" one, the "known" one, everything counts. He is confronted. There is no longer a chance for taking refuge in a state of anonymity without obligation. Through the *knowing* aspect of the election, the symbolic meaning of the singled-out people moves over from the individual to individuation. This point requires, however, more specific elaboration and proof, such as are provided by passages dealing with the election through its connection with *the exodus from Egypt and its symbolic content.*

In many passages concerning the idea of chosenness, and precisely in the most essential ones, reference is made to Yahweh as redeemer of the people from Egypt. Thus continuing our quotation from Deuteronomy 7:6ff., the main passage for the revelation of election, we find the following:

> It was not because you were more in
> number than any other people that the
> Lord set his love upon you and chose
> you, for you were the fewest of all
> peoples; but it is because the Lord
> loves you, and is keeping the oath which
> he swore to your fathers, *that the Lord*
> *has brought you out with a mighty hand,*
> *and redeemed you from the house of*
> *bondage, from the hand of Pharaoh king*
> *of Egypt.*

(Italics mine)

Another highly significant passage in this connection — significant because it unites several elements of the phenomenon of election — is Exodus 6:7:

> ...and I will take you for my people,
> and I will be your God; and you shall

know that I am the Lord your God, *who
has brought you out from under the burdens
of the Egyptians.*

(Italics mine)

Here a new correspondence in the connection between God and
people, in addition to the primary one of being singled out (holiness),
enters into the picture: Yahweh *knows* (chooses) the people *so that
it may know him.* Suggested here is the idea, also to be found in other
Old Testament passages, that God needs his vis-à-vis in order to become
conscious of himself. This could not be stated more clearly than in
Isaiah 48:9-11:

For my name's sake I defer my anger...

. . . . .

Behold, I have refined you, but not like silver;
    I have tried you in the furnace of affliction.
For my own sake, for my own sake, I do it...

(Italics mine)

The word for "tried" is here *bāḥar.* It is commonly assumed that this
second meaning for *bāḥar,* "to test," has nothing to do with the first,
but is rather an Aramaism that corresponds to the Hebrew *bāḥan,* "to
test." It seems to me, however, that the concepts are not so radically far
apart. Choosing in the sense of "singling out" fits very well as a parallel
to "refining" and "trying." Being chosen *is* a matter of being refined
in the "furnace of affliction." Thus, Isaiah 1:25:

I will turn my hand against you
    and will smelt away your dross with lye
    and remove all your alloy.

From Yahweh's insight, "for my own sake, for my own sake, I do it,"

23

we see that Israel's fate is also God's fate. A Midrash to Psalm 91:16,

> With long life I will satisfy him,
> and show him *my salvation.*

(Italics mine)

expresses this plainly: "This is one of the difficult verses, which identify God's salvation with the salvation of Israel."[22]

Thus it is for God's sake that the people shall know him; it shall become conscious of him as the one who led it out of Egypt.

It is now necessary to go carefully into the symbolic content of the exodus motif in connection with the idea of the election. This will be our task in the next lecture.

I I

Last time we investigated the purpose and consequences of the election, starting from an analysis of the verb *bāḥar,* "to choose," and its synonyms and parallel concepts, such as "to grasp," "to cling to someone," "to love," "to desire," "to become aware of," "to fetch," and "to call," all of which brought to light the distinctly irrational-emotional character of the divine choice. We found that Yahweh chose Israel from among all the peoples for *himself,* in order to make it *the people of his own possession,* or *inheritance,* or *portion;* these concepts reveal in the choice of God a claim on the chosen people which is deeply grounded in his being, and a fatefulness both for the chooser and the chosen. The immediate purpose of the choice, as revealed by the texts, is that Israel shall be an *'am qādōš,* a *holy people,* i.e., taking the original Hebrew sense of the word, a *singled-out* people. The *condition* of the election is that the people hold to the commandments of Yahweh and walk in

his ways, thus dedicating themselves to God and sanctifying life, i.e.,
living by a law other than only the law of nature, living in moral conflict, which is the presupposition of becoming conscious.

On the question of Yahweh's ultimate inner motivation for making
a people a holy people, we found the answer in Leviticus 21:8:

> ...for I the Lord, who sanctify you,
>   am holy.

Because Yahweh is himself holy, singled out from all the other gods, the
people, correspondingly, must be holy. The God Yahweh, grown together
as it were out of many polytheistic god-figures into one God-*personality*
and having thereby become *distinct,* chooses for himself a people equally
distinct as his vis-á-vis. Projected onto a people as a collective individual,
we see here the birth of the idea of the individual, i.e., one who steps
out of the anonymity of the cycle of nature into a personal, unique fate.
The consequence of having become distinct is *being meant.* For the one
called, the one known, everything counts, as we saw in a profound passage from Amos:

> You only have I known
>   of all the families of the earth;
>   *therefore I will punish you*
>   *for all your iniquities.*

> (Amos 3:2, italics mine)

The chosen one is confronted. There is no longer a chance for him
to take refuge in a state of anonymity without obligation. Through the
knowing aspect of the election, the symbolic meaning of the singled-
out, i.e., holy, people moves over from the individual to individuation.
This becomes clear as the connection of the election with the exodus
from Egypt enters the picture. Precisely the most essential election pas-

sages show, in immediate connection with the election, a reference to Yahweh as the redeemer of the people from Egypt. Thus, in the key passage
of the election idea, which I would like to repeat, we find the following:

> It was not because you were more in
> number than any other peoples that the
> Lord set his love upon you and chose you,
> for you were the fewest of all peoples;
> but it is because the Lord loves you,
> and is keeping the oath which he swore
> to your fathers, *that the Lord has*
> *brought you out with a mighty hand,*
> *and redeemed you from the house of*
> *bondage, from the hand of Pharaoh*
> *king of Egypt.*

(Deut. 7:7-8, italics mine)

Exodus 6:7 goes a step further:

> ...and I will take you for my people,
> and I will be your God; and *you shall*
> *know that I am the Lord your God, who*
> *has brought you out from under the*
> *burdens of the Egyptians.*

(Italics mine)

This passage makes it clear that Yahweh chooses the people *so that it*
may know him. And, finally, we found this fundamental idea of the Old
Testament pronounced by Yahweh himself:

> For my name's sake I defer my anger...
>
>   .   .   .   .   .
>
> Behold, I have refined you, but not like silver;

26

> I have tried you in the furnace of affliction.
> *For my own sake, for my own sake, I do it...*

(Isaiah 48:9-11, italics mine)

Israel's fate is shown here to be intimately bound up, indeed identical with God's fate. For the sake of God the people shall acknowledge him — *as the one who led it out of Egypt.*

We want to turn now to the symbolic content of the exodus motif in its connection with the idea of election; but, in order to penetrate into the meaning and symbolic content of this divine act of rescuing the people from Egypt, we must pay some attention to the terms that designate this act of redemption.

The most frequently used term is *hōṣî*, "to lead out." A parallel term is *pādā*, "to redeem," actually "to ransom." Thus it says in our main passage, Deuteronomy 7:8:

> ...the Lord has brought you out *(hōṣî)*
> with a mighty hand, and redeemed *(pādā)*
> you from the house of bondage...

Pādā is originally a juridical term, meaning "to ransom" in a concrete sense; in a figurative sense it means to redeem from a miserable condition, from imprisonment as above ("from the house of bondage"), or from the death penalty, as in I Samuel 14:45 where the people "ransom" Jonathan. This understanding of redemption as a deliverance from death will turn up again in connection with the election event.

Pādā occurs more than once as the term expressing rescue from Egypt. Only a few examples will be mentioned:

> And I prayed to the Lord, "O Lord God,
> destroy not thy people and thy heritage,

27

whom thou hast *redeemed (pādītā)* through
thy greatness, whom thou hast brought
out of Egypt with a mighty hand."

(Deut. 9:26, italics mine)

For the Lord has *ransomed (pādā)* Jacob,
  and has redeemed him from hands
    too strong for him.

(Jer. 31:11, italics mine)

Here again Jacob is the embodiment of the whole people.

...but you shall remember that you
were a slave in Egypt and the Lord
your God *redeemed (pādā)* you from there.

(Deut. 24:18, italics mine)

Thus it was *slaves* whom God took for himself as his vis-à-vis by rescuing
them from enslavement.

Frequently we also find *qānā* used as a term expressing election in a
wider sense. It means "to buy," "to acquire," as in Exodus 15:16:

...till thy people, O Lord, pass by
  till the people pass by whom
    thou hast purchased *(qānītā).*

Especially significant is Psalm 74:2:

Remember thy congregation, which
  thou hast gotten (qānītā) of old,

28

> which *thou hast redeemed to be*
> *the tribe of thy heritage!*

> (Italics mine)

No other motif of early Israelite history left behind in the Old Testament such a pervasive and deep impression as the exodus from Egypt. The prophets hammer it into the people, and in Deuteronomy it constitutes the grounds for the commandment, also meant for slaves, to rest on the Sabbath:

> You shall remember that you were a
> servant in the land of Egypt, and the
> Lord your God brought you out thence
> with a mighty hand and an outstretched
> arm; therefore the Lord your God com-
> manded you to keep the Sabbath day.

> (Deut. 5:15)

And:

> You shall not pervert the justice due
> to the sojourner or to the fatherless,
> or take a widow's garment in pledge;
> but you shall remember that you were
> a slave in Egypt and the Lord your God
> redeemed you from there; therefore I
> command you to do this.

> (Deut. 24:17-18)

From generation to generation father shall tell son on Passover night the story of the exodus from Egypt, and a late tradition states that every single Jew must experience this story *as if he himself* had been freed from Egypt.

This commandment never to forget the slavery from which one has escaped seems to me to be very noteworthy from a psychological point of view. Only a free man can afford to remember that he was once a slave; indeed, freedom would even lose its meaning were it separated from the experience of the original darkness of slavery.

In order to grasp the essence of this captivity it is necessary to understand the symbolic meaning of *Egypt* in the Old Testament. One symbolic designation for Egypt, which occurs in only a few passages but proves to be fruitful, is *Rahab:*

> Among those who know me
> I mention Rahab and Babylon...
>
> (Psalm 87:4)

From the parallelism it is quite clear that Egypt is meant by the name Rahab. In Isaiah 30:7 we read:

> For Egypt's help is worthless and empty,
> therefore I have called her
> "Rahab who sits still."

Literally it is: "therefore I call it Rahab." The additional words *hēm šābet* are hard to understand; they mean something like: "they sit still" or "they are still-sitting." It might best be translated as the Zürich Bible does it with "Rahab, brought to silence."

This makes excellent sense in the context of our thoughts, since in other passages Rahab appears implicitly as a synonym for the Babylonian maternal sea monster, *Tiamat.* Thus in Psalm 89:9-10 we find:

> Thou dost rule the raging of the *sea;*
>> when its waves rise, thou stillest them.
> Thou didst *crush Rahab* like a carcass,
>> thou didst scatter thy enemies with thy
>>> mighty arm.

(Italics mine)

Here we see Yahweh in the role of Marduk, conquering the sea monster Tiamat as in the Babylonian creation epic *Enuma-Elish.* This is also the case in Job 26:12:

> By his power he stilled the *sea,*
>> by his understanding *(tebūnā)* he smote *Rahab.*

(Italics mine)

This passage portrays in an especially revealing way the symbolism . of consciousness overcoming the maternal sea monster. Arrow and winds, with which Marduk slays Tiamat, are here replaced by the meaning which they symbolize: Yahweh smote Rahab by his *understanding (tebūnā).* In this Hebrew word the old imagery is still preserved, for *tebūnā* is a derivative of *bēn,* "between," from which is derived *hēbīn,* "to discriminate," "to understand." So we see that *tebūnā* ("understanding") in its original sense means division, differentiation, discrimination. When compared to the Babylonian prototype, this passage offers a rare example of the growing development of consciousness.

Another passage from Job (9:13) gives further evidence of the equivalence of Rahab and Tiamat. In it the "helpers of Rahab" are mentioned, in exact correspondence to the "helpers of Tiamat" in the *Enuma-Elish.*

Thus Israel's captivity in Egypt is a matter of *captivity by Rahab,* imprisonment in the darkness of the devouring maternal unconscious. Out of this Yahweh leads the people, ransoms it, in order to make it "the people of his possession." That this event carries the symbolism of emerging consciousness is expressed especially in Isaiah 51:9-10. There the exodus itself is equated with the world- and consciousness-creating battle of Marduk, beyond that also with the overcoming of the primeval flood, whose symbolic meaning of rescuing consciousness is likewise evident. The passage reads:

> Was it not thou that didst *cut Rahab* in pieces,
>   that didst pierce the dragon?
> Was it not thou that didst dry up the sea,
>   *the waters of the great deep;*
>   *that didst make the depths of the sea a way*
>   *for the redeemed to pass over?*

(Italics mine)

Something highly significant lies hidden in this recital of events: not only is the passage through the Red Sea added as a third motif to the unambiguously mythological events of the conquest over Rahab and the drying up of the primeval flood, but through inner association with the Marduk myth the conquest over Rahab is understood also as a world-creating act, because Marduk created heaven and earth out of the two parts of the conquered Tiamat. The other two events, therefore, namely the drying up of the primeval flood and the deliverance of Israel from Egypt, advance to the rank of *creative acts. We see here a continuity of progressing creative acts.*

To what extent the exodus from Egypt also has the character of a spiritual creation will yet be confirmed by the details of the symbolism. And, as in all flood sagas, the rescued hero comes to a *mountain,* which symbolizes the emergence of consciousness from the waters of the un-conscious, so the delivered people come *through the divided waters to Mount Sinai.* But we are still in Egypt and have to turn to the individu-ation symbolism of the motifs preceding the exodus. In doing this I must, however, sacrifice completeness and select only a few stages.

In the time of greatest affliction at the hands of the Egyptians, the hero Moses appears. His life exhibits typical aspects of the hero's fate: like Herakles and the Babylonian King Sargon I, he is exposed after his birth and he escapes the collective fate of the firstborn sons, i.e., the decimation of the masculine principle. Also the motif of two mothers is present: in Pharaoh's daughter, who takes care of the exposed child, one can, in view of the Pharaoh's closeness to the gods, easily recognize the divine mother of the heroic child.

The turning towards liberation takes place in Moses: turning against the oppressive power, he kills the Egyptian taskmaster and flees from Egypt. The land of Midian into which he journeys is thought to be the place of origin for the Yahweh cult. Here he experiences the first revelation of God. And he marries Zipporah, who then in a very mysterious way knows how to deal with the demonic God Yahweh when he wants to kill Moses, his chosen one, in the night, on the way (Ex. 4:24-26).

The vision of the burning bush can be understood as a symbol of that spiritual passion which seizes without consuming: Moses himself is seized by it. His election as leader of the people shows its authenticity — one finds this mark in all genuine elections — in that it first meets the resistance of the natural man. Thus Moses says: "Oh, my Lord, send, I pray, another person" (Ex. 4:13). Closer to the Hebrew text, the Zürich Bible translates it: "Oh, my Lord, please send whom you want to send" (meant is: only not me).

In the episodes of the transformation of the rod (a positive symbol of the leader) into a serpent and the covering of Moses' hand with leprosy (Ex. 4:1ff) may be seen the intimation of a deadly warning, that he who persists in doubt and declines the election might be exposed to just such a threat and dissociation. We shall return to this death aspect of the declined election in relation to the election of the people.

33

Moses is a chosen one, but in the legend he has divine features. *Mose cornutus,* the horned Moses, of the Vulgate is derived from his illuminated countenance as he descends from Sinai (Ex. 34:29). The Hebrew word *qeren* means both horn and ray. Moses, as the exponent of the people, experiences the revelation of God. In the tradition he is correspondingly called the greatest of the prophets.

> And there has not arisen a prophet since
> in Israel like Moses, whom the Lord knew
> face to face, none like him for all the
> signs and wonders which the Lord sent him
> to do in the Land of Egypt, to Pharaoh and
> to all his servants and to all his land,
> and for all the mighty power and all
> the great and terrible deeds which Moses
> wrought in the sight of all Israel.

(Deut. 34:10-12)

It was Moses' task to lead the whole people to Mount Sinai; this signifies psychologically including *the unconscious powers in the process of becoming conscious.* The people are still in Egypt, still contaminated with the unconscious, still slave to the great mother. In the course of events they reveal themselves as a resisting, stiff-necked people who do not want to become conscious, who demonstrate the resistance of the natural man against the *opus contra naturam,* and who again and again make life go sour for Moses with his higher consciousness. As we shall see, the stiff-necked people express resentment against the process of becoming conscious, similar to that which breaks through in Enkidu in the Gilgamish epic.

But let us turn first to the central episode of the exodus itself, *the passage through the Red Sea.* One finds in the literature a general perplexity over the geographical locale of this passage. Many scholars have been happy to reduce this miraculous event to the completely natural phenomenon of ebb and flood in the Sirbonian Sea at the southern Sinai Peninsula, to which the ebb and flood of the Red Sea were supposed to have stretched.

How they have extricated themselves from the problem of the pillars of cloud and fire, which led the people by day and night respectively, may be shown by two especially striking examples. Kautzsch in his commentary on this passage says: "The conception makes a mockery of every natural explanation; that they are connected with the well-attested customs of smoke and fire signals is at least possible." [23] And Hugo Gressman states that not only the pillars of cloud and fire, but also the catastrophe at the Red Sea, were volcanic in nature.[24] Gressman continues: "All the details of the event, above all also the passage through the sea, must be abandoned"! Thereby, the problem is indeed literally and radically swept under the carpet; at the same time, the deficiency in symbolic thinking sinks to its nadir.

Should it still require proof that the dividing of the waters is an archetypal event, other Old Testament passages can be brought forward to supply this evidence. For example, we have II Kings 2:8 where Elijah, before being carried off to heaven, divides the waters of the Jordan with his cloak in order to pass through with Elisha, and II Kings 2:14 where Elisha on the way back divides the water in the same way. Especially impressive is Joshua 3:14-17:

> So, when the people set out from their
> tents, to pass over the Jordan with the
> priests, bearing the ark of the covenant
> before the people, and when those who bore
> the ark had come to the Jordan, and the
> feet of the priests bearing the ark were
> dipped in the brink of the water (the Jordan
> overflows all its banks throughout the time
> of harvest), *the waters coming down from*
> *above stood and rose up in a heap far off,*

at Adam, the city that is beside Zarethan,
and those flowing down toward the sea of
the Arabah, the Salt Sea, were wholly cut
off; and the people passed over opposite
Jericho. And while all Israel were passing
over on dry ground, the priests who bore
the ark of the Lord stood on dry ground
in the midst of the Jordan, until all the
nation finished passing over the Jordan.

(Italics mine)

Preceding this event was Yahweh's order to Joshua:

"And you shall command the priests who bear
the ark of the covenant, 'When you come to
the brink of the waters of the Jordan, you
shall stand still in the Jordan.'" And Joshua
said to the people of Israel, "Come hither,
and hear the words of the Lord your God."
And Joshua said, "Hereby you shall know
that the living God is among you...Behold,
the ark of the covenant of the Lord is to
pass over before you into the Jordan."

(Joshua 3:8-11)

In our passage, Exodus 14:16-21, the splitting of the sea occurs
when Moses, at the command of God, lifts up his rod and stretches out
his hand; in addition God sends *the east wind,* a symbol of the spirit
of a new consciousness.

The phases of the people's rebellion against the new state of affairs
are most revealing. This rebelliousness breaks out even before they cross
the Red Sea. In Exodus 14:11-12 the people say to Moses:

36

> "Is it because there are no graves in
> Egypt that you have taken us away to
> die in the wilderness? What have you
> done to us, in bringing us out of
> Egypt? Is not this what we said to
> you in Egypt, 'Let us alone and let
> us serve the Egyptians?' For it
> would have been better for us to
> serve the Egyptians than to die in
> the wilderness."

If one compares the wilderness with the satiated unconsciousness
of the Egyptian house of slavery, it has something prospective about it
in that it signifies being ultimately confronted without any possibility
of evasion. It is the symbol of a more conscious suffering which inevitably compels an encounter with the greater. It is the emptiness before
fullness, the privation before fulfillment. Not surprisingly, therefore,
it appears in the prophets as the place of the purest, most original revelation of God, as, for example, in Hosea 9:10:
in Hosea 9:10:

> Like grapes in the wilderness,
>   I found Israel.
> Like the first fruit on the fig tree,
>   in its first season,
>   I saw your fathers.

It is also implied in Hosea 11:1:

> When Israel was a child, I loved him,
> and out of Egypt I called my son.

Also in Jeremiah 2:2-3:

Thus says the Lord,
I remember the devotion of your youth,
    your love as a bride,
how you followed me in the wilderness,
    in the land not sown.
Israel was holy to the Lord,
    the first fruits of his harvest.

With the second outbreak of reproaches against Moses, a menacingly negative projection falls on him and Aaron:

Would that we had died by the hand of
the Lord in the land of Egypt, when we
sat by the fleshpots and ate bread to
the full; for you have brought us out
into this wilderness to kill this whole
assembly with hunger.

(Ex. 16:3)

A third repetition of these complaints drives Moses to a desperate lament: "What shall I do with this people?   They are almost ready to stone me" (Ex. 17:4). This tenacious clinging to unconsciousness and these repeated regressions serve all the more to show the act of becoming conscious in the light of a miracle.

The event at Mount Sinai is extraordinarily numinous. Even to touch the mountain on which Yahweh and Moses meet is fatal for the uninitiated. The *numinosum* is energy of the highest intensity; it can be mortally dangerous, as shown by the example of Uzzah who touched the ark, wanting to prevent it from falling off the wagon, and was killed (II Sam. 6:6ff).

This epoch-making encounter between God and man takes place amidst thunder and lightning, symbols of inner shakenness and illumination. And the sound of the Shofar (ram's horn), which even today is still an

38

extraordinarily numinous symbol of God's call in the ritual of the Day
of Atonement, makes the people tremble. It is onto such churned-up
soul-ground that the moral law falls.

The people are led out of the maternal *primeval waters* through the
wilderness to *Mount Sinai,* in order to receive there the revelation of the
fire-God Yahweh. Such is the price the people must pay for liberation.
Expelled from a vegetative existence in nature and placed in moral conflict, the people must distinguish between good and evil. This is its being
singled out, its being chosen. Here begins the history of suffering for
the sake of consciousness. The election proves to be a tremendous task,
reaching to the limits of human capacity.

In the historical sequence, the people took the pronouncement of
election in a light spirit, looking on it as a guarantee of everlasting well-
being. Hubris lifted its head:

> Evil shall not overtake or meet us.

> (Amos 9:10)

> Is not the Lord in the midst of us?
> No evil shall come upon us.

> (Micah 3:11)

The *condition* for being chosen is forgotten or repressed, and this can
lead to an inner split. This danger comes acutely to the fore in Jeremiah
7:9-10, where Yahweh reproaches the people through his prophet:

> Will you steal, murder, commit adultery,
> swear falsely, burn incense to Ba'al, and
> go after other gods that you have not known,
> and then come and stand before me in this
> house [i.e., the temple], which is called by my name, and

39

say, "We are delivered" — only to go on
doing all these abominations?

Against this hubris of the people the prophets proclaim God's demand
as *the condition for being chosen* and unsparingly remove the grounds
for every form of a soft, non-obligatory concept of the election. Most
rigorous of all is Amos:

> "Are you not like the Ethiopians to me,
>   O people of Israel? " says the Lord.
> "Did I not bring up Israel from the land of Egypt,
>   and the Philistines from Caphtor
>   and the Syrians from Kir? "

> (Amos 9:7)

*The exodus alone is thus in no way a warrant for the belief in being
chosen:* that Israel shares with other peoples. Only through acceptance
of *servitude to God* is the election vouchsafed.

The concept of *the servant of God* comes up repeatedly, therefore,
as a synonym for "the chosen one," as in Isaiah 42:1:

> Behold my servant *('ebed),* whom I uphold,
>   my *chosen (bāḥir),* in whom my soul delights.

> (Italics mine)

Isaiah 65:9 reiterates this point:

> My *chosen* shall inherit it [the land],
>   and my *servants* shall dwell there.

One could cite more passages in this vein.

40

In the so-called Songs of the Servant of God *('Ebed Yahweh)* in Deutero-Isaiah, the Old Testament idea of the chosen people finds its fullest expression. It is not mere chance that many interpreters have identified God's Servant with single historical persons (Moses, Jeremiah, etc.), with the people of Israel, and with the Messiah. The Servant of God is *simply man.* In the manifold meanings ascribable to the Servant of God in these songs, the Old Testament really breaks through its collective conception according to which the people alone is "the chosen one." Each individual, if he puts himself under the election, is the people, just as each also, in that late Jewish tradition, was led out of Egypt.

Returning to our initial question, why God chose one single people, we see from the inner dynamics of the total election event that it *had* to be *some people,* for God's sake. That it was *Israel* may be related to its difficult situation, which prepared it to follow an *inner* way. It was a poor peasant people, eternally oppressed by the surrounding great kingdoms, Egypt and Babylon: It could make room for itself only inwardly, and was thereby peculiarly suited to take upon itself the misery and dignity, the curse and blessing, of God's election. It was, so to speak, *God's easiest prey.* This may be suggested in the motif of the "lowly origin" of the bearer of salvation, as in Deuteronomy 7:6ff where the smallness of the people is pointed out.

Rashi, a medieval commentator, understands *ham-me'at* (the fewest, smallest) not quantitatively but qualitatively.[26] The suitability of Mount Sinai as the mountain of revelation is based by later tradition on its having found favor with God *because it is the lowest* mountain. Similarly the *thorn bush* is God's place of revelation because it is the *least* of all trees.

But that the issue was not that it was precisely this people that was chosen, but that it simply had to be one, anyone, any *one,* which took the election upon itself, comes through very beautifully in a Talmudic

41

passage:

> Jonathan taught: When God said to Hosea that
> Israel had sinned, he expected the prophet to
> defend Israel; instead, Hosea replied: Lord
> of the universe! The whole world belongs to
> Thee. *Replace Israel with another people.* [28]

(Pes. 87b, italics mine)

To my feeling the individuation symbolism of the Biblical idea of the chosen people finds its most profound expression in a Talmudic legend, which relates that God tilted Mount Sinai over the people of Israel like a bucket and said to them:

> If you're willing to receive the Torah,
> good; but if not, here is your grave.

(Trakt. Sabbath 88a)

The claim of the unconscious, if not accepted, leads to a disastrous state of being overwhelmed by the unconscious. A Midrash says:

> Had the Israelites refused, *the world*
> *would have been changed back by God*
> *into an unformed void (Tohu vabohu).*

(Aboda sara 3a, italics mine)

Another version says:

> *The angels would have destroyed the world.*

(Midr. Tehillim 68, 10, italics mine)

Here the election comes into full light as a consciousness-creating phenomenon, for had man not accepted it, the world would have dissolved back into its original unconscious state.

Thus man, as God's partner, guarantees the world's continuance. This idea is also expressed in a kabalistic teaching based on a sentence in Proverbs (10:25), according to which the Zaddik, the pious one, corresponds to the *sefirah Yesod* and thus represents the foundation of the world.

ooooooooooooooooooooooooooooooooo

NOTES

1. M. Freudenthal, *Monatsschrift für Geschichte und Wissenschaft des Judentums,* 1926, p. 338.

2. Compare the same tendency, although in a more moderate form, in the article entitled "The Chosen People" in the *Jewish Encyclopedia.*

3. Jizchak Heinemann, "Behirat 'am Yiśrā'ēl be-miqrā' " ("The Election of Israel in the Bible"), Sinai, 1950, p. 29.

4. Robert Smend, *Lehrbuch der alttestamentlichen Religionsgeschichte,* 1893, pp. 294, 364.

5. G. Quell, *Handwörterbuch des Neuen Testaments,* Vol. IV, p. 169, n. 95.

6. H. H. Rowley, *The Biblical Doctrine of Election,* London, 1950, p. 15.

7. Th. Vriezen, *Die Erwählung Israels im Alten Testament,* Zwingli Verlag, Zürich, 1953.

8. Kurt Galling, *Die Erwählungstraditionen Israels,* Giessen, 1928.

9. H. H. Rowley, op. cit., p. 2, n. 1.

10. G. Quell, op. cit.

11. Jizchak Heinemann, op. cit.

12. G. Quell, op. cit., p. 170.

13. Compare also Staerk, in *Zeitschrift für die alttestamentliche Wissenschaft,* 1937, p. 2; also J. Hempel, *Gott und Mensch im Alten Testament,* 1936, cited by J. Heinemann, op. cit., p. 25.

14. H. H. Rowley, op. cit., p. 35.

15. G. Quell, op. cit., p. 158, n. 5.

16. Ibid., p. 170.

17. Ibid.

18. Jizchak Heinemann, op. cit., p. 18.

19. G. Quell, op. cit., p. 152.

20. Rivkah Schärf Kluger, *Satan in the Old Testament,* Northwestern University Press, 1967, p. 132.

21. In contrast to Quell's interpretation compare Eberhard Baumann, *"Yāda'* und seine Derivate" ("*Yāda'* and its Derivatives"), *Zeitschrift für die alttestamentliche Wissenschaft,* 1908, Vol. 28, p. 110ff.

22. Cf., the article, "Chosen People" in *The Universal Jewish Encyclopedia.*

23. E. Kautzsch, *Die Heilige Schrift des Alten Testaments,* Vol. I, p. 117.

24. H. Gressman, *Anfänge der Israelitischen Geschichte,* p. 56.

25. Cf., Hans Joachim Schoeps, "Agadisches zur Auserwählung Israels," in *Coniectanea Neutestamentica,* Uppsala, 1942, p. 57.

26. Ibid., n. 5.

27. Ibid.

KING SAUL

AND THE SPIRIT OF GOD

PREFATORY NOTE

KING SAUL AND THE SPIRIT OF GOD

"King Saul and the Spirit of God" was a lecture
given in German to the Psychological Club in
Zürich in July 1944 and in English to the Analytical Psychology Club of London, appearing in
print as Guild of Pastoral Psychology, Pamphlet
No. 47 (1947). It was reprinted in *Spring* 1948,
from which this version has been taken. In 1948
the lecture also appeared in German, "Saul und
der Geist Gottes: Ein Beitrag zum Problem der
Melancholie" in *Studien zur analytischen Psy-
chologie C. G. Jungs: Festschrift zum 80. Ge-
burtstag von C. G. Jung,* Zürich: Rascher, 1955.

The translation was made by the author with the
kind collaboration of Barbara Hannah.

INTRODUCTION

The book of Samuel, one of the earliest Biblical texts, is generally assumed to date from the latter half of King David's reign, that is, from
the tenth century B.C. King Saul reigned from about 1030 to 1011,
King David from 1011 to 972. The text, which is by no means uniform,
is composed of different layers of historical and legendary accounts
which have been worked together by the so-called editor. In some passages this is very evident, for example, in those cases where the editor
tries to harmonize contradictory traditions (e.g., I Sam. 17:15). In
many cases there are two or three contradictory versions of the same event.

Modern exegetic investigation discriminates very strictly between history and legend. There would be no objection to this procedure if scholars did not either consciously or unconsciously depreciate legend. It
is doubtless important to disentangle actual history from the full Biblical account. But historical truth is not the whole truth. To obtain the
full character of a period or a man, we must also consider legend, for
it contains as much truth as history itself. Legend originates in the unconscious and supplements the picture given by history. In some cases
legend is a direct compensation for the conscious point of view. We
shall meet an example of this later. The legends which spring up round
an historical personality (whether they are reported by his contemporaries or attributed to him later) show that he has made a vivid impression
not only on the conscious but also on the unconscious, for the latter is
the fertile soil from which comes every myth or legend. There is therefore nothing accidental about the legendary details which collect round
a personality. Consider, for example, the story of David and Goliath
in II Sam. 21:15-22. Four heroes of David's army are each said to have
slain a gigantic Philistine. One of them, Elhanan from Bethlehem, slew
Goliath from Gath. In later times this story was connected with David,

47

because he was the greater hero. But the story was fundamentally changed. The fight between Elhanan and Goliath, although heroic, is still an event capable of occurring in war. But the unconscious of David's contemporaries, and still more that of later generations, had endowed his figure with the characteristics of the mythical hero and the Messiah. Therefore, when the fight was credited to David, it became a symbolical fight between spirit and matter, the expression of a divine charisma. The very fact that such a legend could arise concerning David seems to me, from the point of view of his psychological picture, just as important as the historical facts. If this applies to a typical motif which occurs in many hero stories, we may be sure that it will apply to the more individual and human characteristics which we shall find in the legends of Saul.

These general reflections explain why I have attached equal importance to historical and legendary material where psychological phenomena are concerned. I have only mentioned the fact that passages are exegetically ascribed to a later date when it seems to me of psychological importance. We must achieve a standpoint in the inner sphere (that is, outside space and time) before we can recognize the equal value of these different accounts and see them as facets of an all-embracing truth.

We come up against the difficulty of many variations of one account (in reality an indication of the richness of its inner meaning) at the very beginning of our story. There are no less than three texts dealing with Saul's election as king, and all three accounts must be considered in order to extract those elements which are of importance for the psychological picture.

SAUL'S ELECTION

Saul is introduced in I Sam. 9:2, as a "choice" and "goodly" young man, the son of a well-to-do man of Benjamin. We read:

...And there was not among the children of Israel a goodlier
person than he: from his shoulders and upward he was higher than any of the people.

While he is looking for his father's lost asses he meets Samuel the seer,
who secretly anoints him by previous divine order to be king of Israel
(I Sam. 10:1). Yahweh says in his revelation to Samuel:

That he may save my people out of the hand of the Philistines: for I have looked upon my people, because their cry
is come unto me.

(I Sam. 9:16)

Saul is described here as the strong brave man who will save the people
from the Philistines' oppression. There is no mention of any inner charis-
matic destiny as king; his charisma as leader is only suggested by the
fact that he is anointed by Samuel.

Saul's reaction to the election is similar to that of Moses (Ex. 3:11ff),
that is, surprise and reluctance. Moses exclaims:

Who am I that I should go unto Pharaoh, and that I should
bring forth the children of Israel out of Egypt?

Saul speaks with the same feeling of inferiority when he says (I Sam.
9:21):

Am not I a Benjamite, of the smallest of the tribes of Israel?
and my family the least of all the families of the tribe of
Benjamin? [1]

Moses' reaction expresses not only modesty, but a real uneasiness and
reluctance to accept the mission which led him, after several vain objec-

49

tions, to cry out desperately:

> O my Lord, send, I pray Thee, by the hand of him whom
> Thou wilt send (That is: Please send anyone but me!).

But Saul reacts differently. He follows up his modest protest with the words:

> Wherefore then speakest Thou so to me?

He seems to suspect already the temptation lying in wait for him in election to worldly power. Saul's later fate justifies the hidden fear in these words.

When we consider the corresponding account of David's election as king (I Sam. 16:1-13), we see the essential differences clearly. In Saul's case his outward appearance is emphasized, whereas in David's case God says to Samuel (I Sam. 16:7), who first thought of Eliab, David's brother, as "the Lord's anointed":

> Look not on his countenance, or on the height of his stature;
> because I have refused him: for the Lord seeth not as man
> seeth; for man looketh on the outward appearance, but the
> Lord looketh on the heart.

I think we may assume that there is a connection between these words and the account of Saul's election in Chapter 9. Evidently Yahweh did not choose Saul for his royal appearance; it is the people, and not Yahweh, who judge by externals. Here is an evident contrast between the points of view of God and man on the election of the king. It is the difference between inner and external values, a difference which will prove important in the future development of our subject. Yet David's outward appearance is also mentioned:

50

Now he was ruddy, and withal of a beautiful countenance, and
goodly to look to.

(I Sam. 16:12)

But this plays only a minor role in the election. This is evident not
only from Verse 7 (quoted above), but more particularly from the fact
that the principal emphasis in the story is obviously on another point.

THE RUAH YAHWEH

In Verse 13, we read:

Then Samuel took the horn of oil, and anointed him in the midst
of his brethren: and the Spirit of the Lord came upon David from
that day forward.

This is the true token of charisma: the Ruah Yahweh, the Spirit of God,
which "came upon David from that day forward." In his book, *Der
Geist Gottes und die verwandten Erscheinungen im Alten Testament und
im anschliessenden Judentum,* [2] Paul Volz mentions the following as
manifestations of the Ruah Yahweh: ecstatic rage, *furor bellicus,* gigantic strength and prophecy. I do not, however, regard this as a complete
list of the effects which the Ruah Yahweh can have on man, as the example of David shows us. Judging by this story, I should say that David
was not overcome by the Ruah Yahweh as an exceptional condition;
there is no question here of obsession. For David the Ruah Yahweh
meant divine bliss. Later Judaism speaks of the Shekhinah in the same
way, as a hypostatic inherence of God which comes to rest upon a man.
There is in fact a Talmudic legend which tells how the Shekhinah rested
upon David, though it only expresses this indirectly. [3] A man so affected
is carried by the Ruah Yahweh. He reposes safely with God, and succeeds
in life by God's grace. God's bliss visibly and sensibly rests upon him and

makes him something special. But nothing of this kind is said of the Ruaḥ Yahweh in the story of Saul's election, as I have already pointed out.

We are, however, told that "the Spirit of the Lord will come upon" Saul. Yet it seems to me that the differences between this story and that of David throw a good deal of light on the differences in the personalities of David and Saul, and are particularly illuminating as regards our main theme, the character of Saul. In the story of Saul, the experience of the Ruaḥ Yahweh is not, as with David, directly connected with the anointing by Samuel; and the Ruaḥ Yahweh does not confer worldly and royal distinction upon Saul, but *prophetic possession.*

The text runs as follows:

> Then Samuel took a vial of oil, and poured it upon his head, and kissed him, and said, Is it not because the Lord hath anointed thee to be captain over his inheritance? When thou art departed from me today, then thou shalt find two men by Rachel's sepulchre in the border of Benjamin at Zelzah; and they will say unto thee, The asses which thou wentest to seek are found; and, lo, thy father hath left the care of the asses, and sorroweth for you, saying, What shall I do for my son? Then shalt thou go on forward from thence, and thou shalt come to the plain of Tabor, and there shall meet thee three men going up to God to Beth-el, one carrying three kids and another carrying three loaves of bread, and another carrying a bottle of wine: and they will salute thee, and give thee two loaves of bread; which thou shalt receive of their hands. After that thou shalt come to the hill of God, where is the garrison of the Philistines: and it shall come to pass, when thou art come thither to the city, that thou shalt meet a company of prophets coming down from the high place with a psaltery, and a tabret, and a pipe, and a harp, before them; and they shall prophesy: *And the Spirit of the*

52

Lord will come upon thee, and thou shalt prophesy with
them, and shalt be turned into another man.

(I Sam. 10:1-6, italics mine)

The word "prophesy" *(hitnabbē)* really means: "the ecstatic utterance of sounds." The root, *nābā,* also means "to bring forth" in Arabic
and is used especially of words. [4] It only began to mean "prophecy"
later. The development of the word also gives us an idea of the development of prophecy from mere ecstasy to delivering divine messages. The
noun, *nābi',* prophet, is also derived from the root *nābā.* It is most important for our investigation that the word, *hitnabbē* is used for Saul's
rage in Chapter 8:10, when he was already the victim of his melancholia.
Perhaps this indicates that Saul's melancholy was already taken to be
connected with his prophetic gift. The same connection, but in the reverse sense, is to be seen in the fact that the prophets *(nebi'im)* are dis-
paragingly called *meshugga,* i.e., "mad." Thus Elisha is called a mad
man (II Kings, 9:11) and Jeremiah also (Jer. 29:26); and Hosea (Hosea
9:7) quotes the *vox populi* as saying:

The prophet is a fool, the spiritual man is mad...

Now, with regard to the inner meaning of our text, after anointing
Saul, Samuel foretells three incidents which will happen on his way home,
incidents which he should consider as signs of the reality of his election
as king of Israel. At least such seems to me the meaning of these signs:
that Saul, when he sees these things happen, should realize that his election is equally certain. It is, therefore, assumed that Saul might be in
doubt, and this is quite understandable when we consider how tremendous his experience was and that he was entirely unprepared for it.
There is no apparent connection between the three signs. The first two
are not even directly connected with Saul's election. Symbolically the
first might express the contrast between Saul's two realities, the divine

53

and the human. On the one hand, he is chosen to be the deliverer and
king of Israel; on the other, he is in a constricted human world, son of a
father who is afraid he is in danger and is worrying about him. These
two realities, however, are already contained in the statement of the two
men, "The asses...are found...," which might indicate that as the future
king he will succeed in his purpose. The second sign, the gift of bread,
might also be understood as a symbolic union of Saul's two realities; i.e.,
as a tribute to the secret king. Both these signs underline the impression
of secrecy in Saul's election. Imperceptible to the outer world, it still
has an influence upon it and produces unconscious appreciation. The
third sign is related far more intimately to Saul's election. Regarded
superficially its greater importance is shown by its longer description.
In contradistinction to the first two, it is not only an outward, but above
all an inward sign: the Ruaḥ Yahweh will come upon Saul and change
him into another man. There is no moral accent on this change. It refers to
ecstasy, to exaltation above previous everyday life. A man who has come
into touch with the Ruaḥ Yahweh has become a different man. This appears most clearly in Judges 6:34. Here the coming of the Ruaḥ Yahweh
upon Gideon is expressed by the word *lābaš*, which means "to put on a
dress" — the Ruaḥ Yahweh put on Gideon as if he were a coat. When this
happens to a man he becomes, as it were, nothing but a raiment for the spirit.

With Saul, therefore, it is not the royal charisma which is announced in
these proceedings, but an experience which corresponds in inner value to
it. Compared with the story of David's election, Saul's experience *takes
the place of* the royal charisma.

The very fact that Saul enters a world where signs occur shows that he
is already inwardly transformed. We read this explicitly in Chapter 10:9:

> And it was so, when he had turned his back to go from
> Samuel, God gave him another heart: and all those signs
> came to pass that day.

54

These signs, which are to prove the reality of his election as king, can only be recognized by him after his heart has been changed.

In Saul's case the anointing is followed by an inner transformation. David, however, is anointed "in the midst of his brethren" (I Sam. 16:13), and we read: "the Spirit of the Lord came upon David from that day forward." Here, the royal charisma and the Ruaḥ Yahweh are directly connected, the Ruaḥ Yahweh expressing itself as the royal charisma in its effects on David's surroundings. That is why the election takes place "in the midst of his brethren." It is not so secret as the election of Saul.

We have here an excellent example of the psychological truth of legends. Most biblical scholars regard the story of David's election as a later account, an intentional interpolation which simply imitated the anointing of Saul. As Saul, the King who was afterwards rejected by God, was anointed, David, the victorious King, must certainly be anointed too. But even if it is intentional imitation, how differently these two accounts emerge from the unconscious! It is just the differences that I have mentioned which seem to me typical of the different characters of the two kings.

KINGSHIP AND PROPHETHOOD

The third of the signs foretold by Samuel, that of the fulfillment of Saul's royal election, is the one which strikes me as of decisive importance. This is confirmed by the fact that the first two are only mentioned once again in passing in Chapter 10:9: "...and all those signs came to pass that day," whereas, of the fulfillment of the third, we have a very detailed account. We read:

> And when they came thither to the hill, behold, a company
> of prophets met him; and *the Spirit of God came upon him*
> *and he prophesied among them.*
>
> (I Sam. 10:10, italics mine)

55

This is the first mention of the completed fact that the Spirit of God came upon Saul; although, as I have already pointed out, this did not make him a *king,* but a *prophet.*

In this story Saul's vocations as king and prophet seem to be connected in a peculiar and secret way: *the election as king presupposes the prophetic experience; on the other hand, prophetic ecstacy is a sign of the election as king.* It seems to me that the key to the riddle of Saul's personality is concealed here: the first effect of his election as king is not outward, but inward. It remains a secret between Saul and Samuel, the seer. In the story of his election the outward sign in Saul's personality is no royal activity, no evidence of power or strength, but prophetic possession. In other words, the royal election is like a symbol for an inner, prophetic election. It is as if Saul had been elected to an inner kingdom, the gift of the Spirit of God. Another incident in the story points the same way, for when Saul returns home he purposely keeps his experiences to himself. When his uncle questions him, he serves up this harmless story:

> And Saul's uncle said unto him and to his servant, Whither went ye? And he said, To seek the asses: and when we saw that they were nowhere, we came to Samuel. And Saul's uncle said, Tell me, I pray thee, what Samuel said unto you. And Saul said unto his uncle, He told us plainly that the asses were found.
>
> (I Sam. 10:14-16)

And then the text actually says:

> But of the matter of the kingdom, whereof Samuel spake, he told him not.
>
> (I Sam. 10:16)

Sellin points out in his *Geschichte des Volkes Israel* (p. 147), that this is in fact a widely encountered fairytale motif: "The hero goes out to search for asses, and finds a royal crown." But in our story the motif seems to acquire greater depth of meaning. From the external point of view Saul found only the asses; the crown, which he had found, remained his inner secret which became a reality for him through the Ruaḥ Yahweh, when he came upon him.

And from this same outward point of view his ecstatic experience is far from representing, as the text shows further on, royal eminence. Verses 11 and 12 of Chapter 10 tell us:

> And it came to pass, when all that knew him beforetime
> saw that, behold, he prophesied among the prophets, then
> the people said one to another, What is this that is come
> unto the son of Kish? Is Saul also among the prophets?
> And one of the same place answered and said, But who is
> their father? Therefore it became a proverb, Is Saul also
> among the prophets?

It is clear from this passage that these prophets were despised socially. For example, the question, "But who is their father? " contrasts the lowly birth of the prophets with that of Saul, whose father is wellknown. The names and homes of the prophets are not mentioned. And if it is astonishing to find an honorable man's son among these prophets, it is still more incomprehensible to find a king. But it seems to me that in this contrast is the very depth of the story. Saul's kingship, which is still a secret, finds exact expression in his insignificant and despised condition, i.e., in his being a member of the group of prophets. As this passage points to the proverb it is, in my opinion, incontrovertible proof that Saul's prophetic gift is an historical fact. The proverb undoubtedly existed. Such complicated and compromising statements are never invented about a king. Another proof of the genuineness of this proverb, and thus of the fact that Saul really had the prophetic gift, is the attempt of another and probably later author to explain the origin of the proverb. This version (I Sam. 19 :18 ff) is less plausibly connected with the preceding story and is less likely to be historical. But it shows characteristics important to our subject, for it contributes to the inner picture of Saul. Moreover it contains valuable details concerning the phenomenon of ecstasy, and I should therefore like to take it into consideration.

Saul finds out that David has escaped to Samuel to the house of the prophets in Ramah. Then we read:

> And Saul sent messengers to take David: and when they
> saw the company of the prophets prophesying, and Samuel
> standing as appointed over them, the Spirit of God was
> upon the messengers of Saul, and they also prophesied.
> And when it was told Saul, he sent other messengers, and
> they prophesied likewise. And Saul sent messengers again
> the third time, and they prophesied also. Then went he
> also to Ramah...
>
> (I Sam. 19:20-22)

He came to a hill, and then we read further:

> And he went thither to Naioth in Ramah: and the Spirit of
> God was upon him also and he went on, and prophesied,
> until he came to Naioth in Ramah. And he stripped off
> his clothes also, and prophesied before Samuel in like man-
> ner, and lay down naked all that day and all that night.
> Wherefore they say, Is Saul also among the prophets?
>
> (I Sam. 19:23-24)

I find it very significant that Samuel is the leader of the ecstatic prophets. Here we have an inner relationship between Samuel and Saul, namely, their common gift of prophecy. The narrative also shows very clearly the contagiousness of ecstasy. But is is a subtle touch that Saul is said to have fallen into ecstasy before he met the prophets, and not, like the messengers, merely by watching the others. With him it is not merely contagion. On the contrary, it is expressly stated that the Spirit of God came upon him while he was on the way. This implies that the experience is no mere accident, but fate.

We find another entirely different version of Saul's royal election, in Chapter 10, 17-27, in which everything happens outside; a public election takes place by lot. This impersonal, almost accidental, election stands in sharp contrast to the very personal one in the first story.

This version is a direct continuation of Chapter 8, where the people of Israel ask Samuel for a king. Yahweh yields. The atmosphere can almost be described as: "Very well then, have your king!" This version, like Chapter 8, belongs to the unhistorical account of the origin of the monarchy, an account which came into being as a result of certain unhappy experiences of monarchy on the part of the people. [5] It is also pertinent that nothing essential is said here about Saul's personality, let alone any mention of the charisma through the Ruah Yahweh. Only Saul's striking height is mentioned.

And yet this version also has a place in the full psychological picture. While the first story shows the inner subjective danger which kingship held for Saul, the second might be said to show the *objective ambivalence* of monarchy as an institution.

In Chapter 8 the people clamor: "But we will have a king over us; that we also may be like all the nations; ..." (I Sam. 8:19-20). Yahweh himself compares this desire of the people with their back sliding into idolatry. He says to Samuel:

...for they have not rejected thee, but they have rejected me, that I should not reign over them. According to all

the works which they have done...wherewith they have
forsaken me, and served other gods...

(Sam. 8:7-8)

One could not speak of kingship in a more negative fashion. It is apostasy regarding God to imitate other nations at the cost of theocracy. Kingship had already been offered by the people to one of the Judges before Saul, namely Gideon. But Gideon answered them:

I will not rule over you, neither shall my son rule over you:
the Lord shall rule over you.

(Judges 8:23)

Yet, in I Samuel 8, side by side with God's decided rejection of the idea of a king, we find an almost incomprehensible command to Samuel to give way to the people's wish. This riddle can perhaps be solved only by a general survey of the Kingdom of Israel. The fact that God gives way to the people's demand seems to suggest the necessity of a kingdom, a necessity which finds full expression in the stories of Saul's anointment. It is evident that though on the one hand God violently refuses the kingdom, on the other he really *wants* it. Even when Saul failed, God did not give up the idea of the kingdom; on the contrary he told Samuel very impatiently to anoint another king! (I Sam. 16:1). In Chapter 8, therefore, it is no mere contradiction, but rather a genuine ambivalence toward the idea of kingship.

What was the real destiny of the kingdom in Israel? It grew up out of the People of Israel's necessity to keep Canaan and to defend themselves against their neighbors. David's kingdom, constantly attacked as it was by its great neighbors, Babylon and Egypt, could not maintain itself. But the idea of the kingdom did not disappear with David. It *grew into the divine realm.* Kingship, as an archetype, became an aspect of the divine personality Yahweh. This is particularly clear in the so-called Yahweh Malak Psalms, which all begin with "Yahweh is king!" But already in II Sam. 7:14, Yahweh wants to establish David's throne forever, for he says of Solomon: "I will be his father, and he shall be my son."[6]

This development of the idea of kingdom may be looked upon as the Old Testament foundation for the theological idea of the kingdom of Christ which is not of this world. In the Old Testament, the Babylonian and Egyptian idea of kingdom ultimately became a symbol of God's kingdom in this world; and the ambivalence in the idea of kingship, which we sense in I Samuel 8, can be recognized as the beginning and the end of this development. A divine necessity was concealed behind what seemed to be God's weakness in giving way to the desires of the people.

This version of the story of Saul's royal election, which is opposed to the idea of the kingdom, is important from a psychological point of view, because this divine impulse to create kingship literally became Saul's fate. He became king by lot, picked out from the anonymous crowd as, so to speak, the mere instrument of an impersonal, superhuman process — an aspect of the election to which I will return.

Let us now turn to the third version, that in which the trouble with the Philistines is the real cause of Saul's election. This version is probably a true record of the outward events. Here Saul is one of the Judges, one of those heroes elected by God whom we find in the Book of Judges: Othniel (3:10), Gideon (6:34 ff), Jephthah (11:29), etc. Saul differs from them only by the fact that he is the first not to disappear after the fulfillment of his task, but to remain and be elected king.

We have heard in the first version also that Saul should save Israel out of the hands of the Philistines. But, as we have seen in that version, the main accent is laid on the inner process of transformation. Both these versions give different aspects of one historical fact, namely, Saul's becoming king over Israel. They seem to me, however, to be two different stories, although there are other opinions in the literature. In this account Saul is not yet king; he is a peasant who comes home from his fields and hears the bad news that the town of Jabesh is threatened by the Ammonites. As a reaction to the pressing need he becomes a leader in the war, and after the victory he becomes king over Israel. In this story also, the Ruah Yahweh, the Spirit of God, is mentioned. Here, however, the Spirit of God which overcomes him is a *furor bellicus,* which can be seen in the archaic form of the summons. We read:

> And he took a yoke of oxen, and hewed them in pieces,
> and sent them throughout all the coasts of Israel by the
> hands of messengers, saying, Whosoever cometh not forth
> after Saul and after Samuel, so shall it be done unto his oxen.
>
> (I Sam. 11:7)

The text continues:

> And the fear of the Lord *(pahad Yahweh)* fell on the people,
> and they came out with one consent.

That the Ruah Yahweh, the Spirit of God, can appear as a *furor bellicus* is not astonishing when we remember all the passages in the Old Testament where Yahweh himself interferes in wars, even in a cruel way.[7] We find a survey of all these passages in Volz's *Das Daemonische in Jahweh.*[8] Yahweh is often actually depicted as a war hero, especially in Isaiah 42:13:

> The Lord shall go forth as a mighty man, he shall stir up
> jealousy like a man of war: he shall cry, yea, roar; he shall
> prevail against his enemies.

But is it not significant that the Ruah Yahweh as a *furor bellicus* is never mentioned in connection with David, who was afterwards the war hero *par excellence* and had far greater success in this respect than Saul? David's enterprises in war were accompanied by perpetual divine bliss, as the story of his election foretells, but his warriorship was never an obsession. We see this very well in the story of Goliath. David is cheerful and serene when he goes out to fight the giant, and has a childlike faith in God. There is nothing demoniacal about it. In a state of obsession it is possible to bring off a great coup but it is not possible to found and maintain a kingdom. Saul is the first of the war heroes who were overcome by the Ruaḥ Yahweh and became king, and in the end he suffered shipwreck.

At the beginning, however, Saul is victorious in war. After the account of the relief of the town Jabesh in Gilead from the Ammonites, there is a long description of his successful wars against the Philistines, in which his son Jonathan particularly distinguished himself as a hero (Chaps. 13 and 14), and Chapter 15 is concerned with Saul's conquest of the Amalekites in the South, an old enemy of Israel.[9]

SAUL'S GUILT

But in these last accounts of victory misfortune is already creeping in. In Chap. 13:7-15 and in Chap. 15 two parallel narratives are fitted in which speak of Saul's guilt and rejection. Both narratives have the same motif: Saul commits a ritual crime and is rejected by God on that account. Both these narratives see the cause of Saul's failure as a *personal guilt*.

The first version is much weaker. Here Saul's guilt consists in the fact that he offered the sacrifice before the battle instead of waiting for Samuel. He did so because the people began to disperse and the Philistines were coming nearer and nearer. Afterwards Samuel says to him:

Thou hast done foolishly: thou hast not kept the command-

63

ment of the Lord thy God, which he commanded thee: for
now would the Lord have established thy kingdom upon
Israel for ever. But now thy kingdom shall not continue:
the Lord hath sought him a man after his own heart, and
the Lord hath commanded him to be captain over his people, because thou hast not kept that which the Lord commanded thee.

(I Sam. 13:13-14)

For many reasons this version was recognized as a later interpolation:
because, for instance, it is not connected with the following events.[10]
In comparison with the second version it contains nothing new from the
psychological point of view; therefore, we seem justified in basing our
considerations on the second alone, which has a much better form.

Saul's guilt, in the second story also, consists of a religious crime; he
is disobedient to the divine command concerning the ban on Amalek.
It seems strange at first that Saul's decisive crime should be such an insignificant, impersonal, merely collective one. The ban means that no
booty was allowed, neither men, animals, nor any other enemy goods
might be spared; everything must be destroyed. Probably originally there
was an old taboo behind it: the enemy (the stranger) must be entirely
destroyed on account of the malignance which might adhere to him and
to everything which belonged to him. [11] The ban here, in its whole archaic cruelty, is an expression of the idea of Yahweh's war, which is not
fought for the sake of outer goods but for Yahweh. The enemy and
everything which belongs to him must be sacrificed. [12] Saul's disobedience to this divine command, therefore, shows that he is no longer related to God and his commands, particularly in his role as king and com-
mander-in-chief. He acts from worldly and covetous reasons. We read:

But Saul and the people spared Agag, and the best of the
sheep, and of the oxen, and of the fatlings, and the lambs,

64

and all that was good, and would not utterly destroy them:
but every thing that was vile and refuse, that they destroyed
utterly.

(I Sam. 15:19, italics mine)

Samuel recognizes this tension in Saul when he says:

Wherefore then, didst thou *not obey the voice of the Lord,*
but didst fly upon the spoil, and didst evil in the sight of
the Lord?

(I Sam. 15:19)

It belongs to Saul's possessed and extreme nature that he was not able
to be king and Yahweh's servant at the same time. His kingship led him
into identification with worldly power. The worldly purposes of the
kingdom detach him from God — that is, *his possession by God turns
into a profane possession.* Thus his crime consists in the fact that he is
now exclusively king in a way which has lost its relation to God. This
idea seems to be contradicted by other narratives, especially by Chapter
14:38 ff,[13] where Saul is prepared to sacrifice his son in rigid fulfillment
of the curse which Jonathan called upon himself by his unconscious
offense in tasting the honey against Saul's command to abstain. Budde
says very aptly about this passage that it gives "an excellent picture of
Saul's melancholic, nervous, religious consciousness."[14] This extreme zeal of Saul's is in fact the exact counterpart of his disobedience
in Chapter 15. Only the man who is latently disobedient needs to be
obedient to such an extreme and absurd degree. Unfree, constrained
obedience has the same root as disobedience. Saul's obedience here does
not come from the center of his human, personal being. We find this
center very beautifully portrayed in the people's attitude. They judge
from *feelings* of love and veneration towards Jonathan. They do not
rigidly pass over the human aspect of the situation for the sake of the

law as such. They find a way to rescue Jonathan and yet to follow the divine law at the same time. [15]

Thus Saul's offense in the religious sphere is deeply rooted in his psychic structure. It is really personal guilt. But here already we can sense something of the tragic aspect of his guilt. It becomes clear that the kingship, to which he was obviously dedicated by God himself, was at the same time *the* great danger, *par excellence* for him, the catastrophic temptation. Here we see the disastrous fulfilment of his anxious foreboding in the first story of his election, when he says to Samuel: "...Wherefore then speakest thou so to me? " (i.e., that I shall become king). So it comes about that God says to Samuel:

> *It repenteth me* that I have set up Saul to be king: for he
> is turned back from following me, and hath not performed
> my commandments.
>
> (I Sam. 15:11, italics mine)

All the weight of this divine decision can be felt in its effect on Samuel. The text continues:

> And it grieved Samuel; and he cried unto the Lord all night.

In the statement of God's repentance concerning Saul's election it seems to me that we can see the confirmation of a really tragic element in Saul's fate. In the end it leads beyond mere human guilt, even to a complicity of God, if one may dare to say such a thing! I will return to this subject at the end. But I do not mean the idea of God's complicity as a contradiction of the fact of Saul's own guilt, just as the text itself does not wash out Saul's personal guilt when it speaks of God's repentance. The two aspects, superhuman and human, do not exclude each other but exist side by side.

Saul's desertion of God is to be seen not only in the fact that he does not carry out the ban, but also in his attitude towards Samuel who calls

him to account. He deceives both Samuel and himself. He greets Samuel
when he arrives as if nothing had happened:

> Blessed be thou of the Lord: I have performed the com-
> mandment of the Lord.
>
> (I Sam. 15:13)

But the inexorable Samuel drives him into a corner:

> What meaneth then this bleating of the sheep in mine ears,
> and the lowing of the oxen which I hear?
>
> (I Sam. 15:14)

Saul tries to escape by saying that the best sheep and oxen have been
spared to sacrifice to God. Moreover, he does not shrink from answering
Samuel's question as to why he did not obey the voice of God:

> Yes, I have obeyed the voice of the Lord, and have gone
> the way which the Lord sent me, and have brought Agag
> the king of Amalek, and have utterly destroyed the Ama-
> lekites. But the people took of the spoil, sheep and oxen,
> the chief of the things which should have been utterly de-
> stroyed, to sacrifice unto the Lord thy God in Gilgal.
>
> (I Sam. 15:20)

Samuel's reproaches are very severe and culminate in the announce-
ment of Saul's rejection (I Sam. 15:22-23). Then Saul pleads guilty:

> I have sinned: for I have transgressed the commandment
> of the Lord, and thy words: because....

— the motive for his deed which follows is very instructive —

...I feared the people, and obeyed their voice.

(I Sam. 15:24)

Here already he is a mistrustful, uncertain, inwardly irritated man who fears the people over whom he should reign. He is no longer at one with his people, no longer at one with himself as king. His royal power is already undermined from within.

In this profound insecurity Saul begs Samuel to return with him. But Samuel says:

I will not return with thee: for thou hast rejected the word of the Lord, and the Lord hath rejected thee from being king over Israel.

(I Sam. 15:26)

Then Samuel turns away to leave. But Saul clings to him and catches hold of the skirt of his mantle till it tears. This little detail seems to me of symbolical importance, not only for the reason given by Samuel himself:

The Lord hath rent the kingdom of Israel from thee this day, and hath given it to a neighbour of thine, that is better than thou.

(I Sam. 15:28)

But it is also an expression of the rent between Samuel and Saul. Samuel embodies Saul's "other side," so to speak. He is a seer, a prophet, and Saul has split himself off from his own prophetic side, the side related to God, by his disobedience and his treason towards Samuel. In the Endor episode with which we must deal later, when Saul meets Samuel's ghost, he meets, as it were, his own detached, split-off side which is related to

68

God. It can, however, only draw him into its own seclusion; he is no longer able to unite with it in life. In this connection it is perhaps interesting that the names Samuel and Saul are traced back to the same root in I Sam. 1:20. According to this passage the name Samuel *(Šemū'ēl)* is derived from *Šā'ül*, which means "asked for." The etymology of this name is not yet clear, and there are many different opinions about it, but the mere fact that in the Bible itself the two names are rightly or wrongly identified is somehow significant in our connection. I should also like to mention that, according to Gesenius' *Hebrew Lexicon,* the root *Šā'ül* also occurs in the name for the realm of the dead *(Se'ōl).* This fact seems significant when we remember Saul's melancholy and his Endor experience. I must admit, though, that this derivation is considered questionable today.

The deep relation between Samuel and Saul, however, can also be felt in the further narrative. Samuel yields to Saul's wish and returns with him, but only in order to execute the ban on Agag, the king of Amalek, that Saul has omitted. Then he leaves Saul for ever. From this time on Saul's fate is sealed and there is really no longer any hope for him. This fact is expressed in a moving way in the last sentence of this significant Chapter 15, where we read:

> And Samuel came no more to see Saul until the day of his death: *nevertheless Samuel mourned for Saul.*
>
> (I Sam. 15:35, italics mine)

Looked at from his Samuel-aspect, Saul is already dead.

THE EVIL SPIRIT OF GOD

Saul had turned away from Yahweh, and now Yahweh turns away from him: he withdraws the charisma which he had once bestowed upon him, and which made him a leader. It was after this event in the life of

Saul that his melancholy began. Now that his desertion from God has become manifest, so to speak, in his disobedience, now that God has rejected him as king, a transformation of the inward side also takes place: the Ruah Yahweh turns into a negative possession; it becomes a *bad demon.* This change is expressed by one short sentence:

> *But the spirit of the Lord departed from Saul, and an evil spirit from the Lord troubled him.*

> (I Sam. 16:14, italics mine)

It is the same spirit of God, but in its evil aspect. This can be seen still more clearly in the following sentence, where an "evil spirit of God": *Ruah 'elōhim rā'ā,* is spoken of directly. The Septuagint shows us that the original word here was Yahweh, not *Elohim,* i.e., *Ruah Yahweh rā'ā,* an evil spirit of Yahweh.[16] It was probably felt in some later age as too shocking and changed, for Yahweh is a higher name for God than Elohim.

The betrayed Spirit of God in Saul torments him as melancholy, as depression, as demented rage or as possession by gloomy ideas. Medical psychologists may perhaps be especially interested in the fact that on account of this passage the term, *rūah rā'ā,* evil spirit, became the technical term for melancholy in later Judaism. The famous doctor and scholar Maimonides, who lived in the 12th century, says literally in his commentary on the Mischnah: "One uses the term 'evil spirit' for all kinds of diseases which are designated as *melancholia* in Arabic." At that time the Greek authors were hardly known except in Arabic translations, and this Mischnah commentary by Maimonides is also written in Arabic and has been translated into Hebrew.

So Saul's melancholy is the negative aspect of possession by the Spirit of God. The fact that the Spirit of God in its negative aspect overcomes Saul like a personal, strange demon shows that it is an inner, objective reality from which Saul is now estranged. To use psychological language, the Ruaḥ Yahweh has become a split-off complex, and therefore falls upon him like a strange *person.* Saul is not able to realize the divine power which is concealed in his suffering. His melancholy is a forlorn psychical condition in which he can no longer hear the voice of God.

One of the most beautiful and significant narratives in the Old Testament contains a counterpart to Saul's attitude — Jacob's wrestling with the man in the night (Gen. 32:24ff). Here also it is a demon that falls upon Jacob, and yet he blesses Jacob, because Jacob struggled with him. And Jacob knew that he had seen God face to face (Gen. 32:30). But what is Saul's attitude? He does not fight. He does not recognize God in the demon but becomes entirely its victim and to a certain extent identical with it. In as far as he is not identical with it he is a hopelessly helpless man who listens to the superficial advice of his servants to expel the evil demon by music. That was how his successor, David, psychologically his exact opposite, came to his court. We read:

> And it came to pass, when the evil spirit from God was
> upon Saul, that David took an harp, and played with
> his hand: so Saul was refreshed *(rāwaḥ),* and was well,
> and the evil spirit departed from him.

> (I Sam. 16:23)

Readers know the wonderful picture by Rembrandt which depicts this scene and expresses Saul's suffering in a really moving way.

The verb *rāwaḥ,* which is used in this passage, means to become wide, airy, and shows clearly the inner connection with the word *rúaḥ.* It is really the same word. By means of music a positive *rúaḥ,* spirit of life, enters into the melancholic, distressed man. He is able for a short time to "breathe" again. Psychologically it is also significant that David is the

71

one who is able to bring about this deliverance. It is to him that the
Ruaḥ Yahweh passes over in its positive aspect as royal charisma. But
he thus inevitably becomes the object of Saul's negative feelings, of his
envy, jealousy and anger. Saul is not able to accept the fate which was
announced to him by Samuel (I Sam. 15:10), that Yahweh has rejected
him as king. He no longer has his place in the order of God's will. He
fights with the rage of despair against David, against the man upon whom
Yahweh's charisma lies. He thus fights against Yahweh himself, not, like
Jacob, in order to be blessed, but in order to carry through his own human will against God's will. He is really driven by the "evil spirit."

The "evil spirit" in him drives him to incredible deeds. Thus he tries
to "smite David even to the wall" with his javelin as he plays the lute
before him, a motif which is repeated twice (I Sam. 18:10 and 19:9).
Then he promises him his elder daughter Merab as his wife, but does not
give her to him (I Sam. 18:17). As the price of his younger daughter
Michal he sends David into the battle against the Philistines, hoping that
he will not return (I Sam. 18:25). Then he tries to have David killed
in his own house (I Sam. 19:11), a fate David was only able to escape
thanks to Michal's love and prudence. Moreover, Saul does not shrink
from killing all the priests of Nob because they were said to have helped
David to escape (I Sam. 22:9 ff, etc.). Occasionally the light of wisdom
breaks through his blind, raging revolt; as, for instance, in the story of
his meeting with David in the hollow of Engedi where David generously
spares his life. Saul's whole great inner trouble can be felt here. The
text says:

> And Saul lifted up his voice, and wept. And he said to
> David, Thou art more righteous than I: for thou hast
> rewarded me good, whereas I have rewarded thee evil.

> (I Sam. 24:16, 17)

But this light of insight is again extinguished. He marches out anew to search for David in the desert of Siph (I Sam. 26) with the purpose of destroying him. Jonathan, Saul's son, who is deeply devoted to David, has the submission to fate which is missing in his father. He bows to David's kingship. Jonathan's whole attitude proves his greatness, for it is not only in this matter that he is generous.

> The Lord do so and much more to Jonathan: but if it please my father to do thee evil, then I will shew it thee, and send thee away, that thou mayest go in peace: and the Lord be with thee, as he hath been with my father.
>
> (I Sam. 20:13)

And a little further on we read:

> And Jonathan caused David to swear again, because he loved him: for he loved him as he loved his own soul.
>
> (I Sam. 20:17)

But is not Saul's incalculableness an expression of his abysmal emotionality, which again is in itself an expression of the Ruaḥ Yahweh in its demoniacal ambivalence? Is it not an image of Yahweh's emotionality, which itself falls from one extreme into the other, from grace to rage? He knows profound pity and justice, but also blind, raging destruction. What else can the *rūaḥ rāʿā mēʾēt Yahweh,* the evil spirit of God, mean but the demoniacal power *in* Yahweh, the demoniacal spirit of Yahweh itself? It is the opposite of Yahweh's light side, from which Saul is cut off by his guilt and rejection.

ENDOR

Saul can no longer be healed; he is no longer able to return. This state leads automatically to the complete breakdown of his inner forces and outward power. It leads him into the realm of the dead before he himself is dead — into his experience with the woman of Endor, which is most meaningful from the psychological point of view. In the end it leads him into physical death, which meant the entire breakdown of his power and throne, for all his sons (except Ishbaal, who was only able to retain the throne for a short time) died with him. Unconsciously Saul thus carried out the divine commandment himself; he had to take all three sons into the battle with him, so that they might all die together. There is a legend which gives him credit for this. It relates:

> The next day (after the experience of Endor) Saul took his three sons Jonathan, Abinadab and Melchishua, and marched out with them into the battle. In that hour the Lord spake to the ministering angels: Behold the hero whom I have created. When a man goes to a festival, he shrinks from taking his children with him, from fear of the evil eye. But this man goes into certain death and takes his three sons with him. He is looking forward to the disastrous fate which will befall him! [17]

This legend is a beautiful compensation for Saul's reversed conscious attitude; for on the conscious side his fate is just what he cannot accept.

Saul's meeting with Samuel's ghost at the house of the woman of Endor shows him in his deepest loneliness. He goes to the woman of Endor to ask her to conjure up Samuel's ghost (Samuel, who was gifted with the Ruaḥ Yahweh) because Saul himself is entirely forsaken by Yahweh. He says to Samuel:

> ...I am sore distressed; for the Philistines make war against me, and *God is departed from me, and answereth me no more, neither by prophets, nor by dreams:* therefore I have called thee, that thou mayest make known unto me what

I shall do.

(I Sam. 28:15, italics mine)

But Samuel can only point back to the pitiless fact of Saul's rejection:

Wherefore then dost thou ask of me, seeing the Lord
is departed from thee, and is become *thine enemy?*

(I Sam. 28:16, italics mine)

This situation is profoundly moving. Moreover, it was Saul himself who, in his zeal for Yahweh, had "put away those that had familiar spirits, and the wizards out of the land." Therefore his inner decay can again be seen very clearly in the fact that he has now himself resorted to a woman who has a familiar spirit. The fact that God has forsaken him leads him into black magic, which is in itself far from God, and his melancholy draws him down, while he is still alive, into the darkness of the realm of death. We must also remember here that, though Saul died in battle, he really committed suicide. He was wounded, and begged his armor-bearer to thrust his sword through him lest the enemy scoff at him; but the armor-bearer refused "for he was sore afraid," as the Bible says, and so Saul threw himself upon the sword. The Philistines then cut off his head, put his armor in the temple of Astarte and fastened his dead body to the wall of Beth-shan. The inhabitants of Jabesh, who had not forgotten Saul's first heroic deed when he saved their town from the Ammonites, fetched his corpse in the night, buried it and mourned for him. Thus Saul's sad end was, as it were, connected with his brilliant beginning.

SAUL'S INSOLUBLE CONFLICT

When we consider the fate of this king in ancient Israel we cannot help being moved by an impression of great tragedy. Saul was thrown into an insoluble conflict between his inner and outer call. His prophetic gift was smothered by his worldly task; but this task itself could not be accomplished, because the divine fire turned into melancholy and disturbed his psychic equilibrium.

The fact that Saul's prophetic gift had *the primitive character of prophetical ecstasy* seems to me also to have played an important role in this tragedy. It was impossible for him to have a consciously religious attitude towards his gift of the Spirit of God. He remained possessed and was unable to reach the level of human decision. A comparision with the great prophets may make this plain. All the great prophets, especially Jeremiah, the ripest and most conscious among them, found the prophetical gift a cause of *suffering*. It excluded them from normal life, drove them into trouble and privation, and brought them persecution and maltreatment. I will mention only the complaint of the *Ebed Yahweh,* the servant of God, in Isaiah 49:4, which belongs to the so-called Deutero-Isaiah:

> ...I have laboured in vain, I have spent my strength for nought, and in vain, ...

and Jeremiah's words:

> I sat not in the assembly of the mockers, nor rejoiced;
> I sat alone because of thy hand: for thou hast filled
> me with indignation.

> (Jeremiah 15:17)

But this suffering does not turn into melancholy, because it is finally accepted as belonging to the gift of the spirit. There are times of despair, even of rebellion, but there is no escaping, because the experience

76

of the fact of being God's servant is stronger. The meaning of suffering is recognized and it is endured. Deutero-Isaiah has expressed this most beautifully. The complaint just noted is immediately followed by certainty:

> ...yet, surely my judgment is with the Lord, and my
> work with my God.
>
> (Isaiah 44:4)

Jeremiah also expresses it:

> Then I said, I will not make mention of him, nor speak
> any more in his name. But his word was in mine heart
> as a burning fire shut up in my bones, and I was weary
> with forbearing, and I could not stay.
>
> (Jeremiah 20:9)

He knows that he *must* speak, because otherwise he would perish, consumed by the inner fire. He is also acquainted with ecstasy, as we hear when he says:

> Mine heart within me is broken because of the prophets; all my bones shake; I am like a drunken man,
> and like a man whom wine hath overcome, because
> of the Lord, and because of the words of his holiness.
>
> (Jeremiah 23:9)

But, in contrast to Saul, he had the great advantage of receiving the Ruah Yahweh as the *word* and not just as demoniacal possession. To the great prophets the Ruah Yahweh is no longer just an emotional but has become a real spiritual possession. Therefore they do not just carry the Ruah Yahweh; they are not only passively seized by it, but it

77

is also a content which challenges them in their human center. In these prophets God is no longer primarily emotion, the burning heat of the soul, but rather a spiritual personality with which they are able to have a human relationship, although it naturally seizes them with its spiritual power.

Saul belonged to the prophetic type of earlier times, and his divine possession turned into melancholy. He was not able, like the great prophets, to transform his possession by God into devotion to God. He was the sinister, mistrustful, lonely man. In contrast, David was the man who was bound up in life and God, and therefore his life and task were successful. But David's nature was not discordant and profound, like that of Saul. Saul was further from God, but also correspondingly nearer. The bliss of God rested upon David, but Saul was marked by God's spirit. David corresponded to the collective ideal of a king, therefore later Jewish folklore and all the corresponding legends connected him with the Messiah. The best-known example is Christ's genealogical tree in which he is descended from the line of David. Had Saul been able to stand his fate, he would never have been a figure which fitted into collective conceptions; he would have become a great *personality*.

GOD'S REPENTANCE

This is perhaps the place to come back to the problem of God's repentance.

When God repents that he made Saul a king, he admits (according to this metaphor) that he has made a mistake from his divine point of view. Could this mistake not consist in the double claim on Saul to be at the same time king and prophet? God thus asked more of Saul than of David, and also more than of the prophets. What could this claim mean *psychologically?* It is the nature of the Ruaḥ Yahweh to lead the prophet out of the world. This can be seen in the fate of Amos, Jeremiah and the second Isaiah. Now the king, if he is only the king, is the extreme opposite of the prophet. He must represent and defend worldly power. He embodies, so to speak, the principle of the world. Therefore God asked a great deal of Saul: he was to keep his feet in the inner world, and at the same time to do full justice to the outer world, which amounts to reconciling the inward and the outward opposites in his own person. Could we not understand this psychologically as a *demand for totality* made by God on the man Saul? But then we must ask, further, what made God demand this?

Here I want to make a suggestion only. The divine idea of wholeness, which seems to be constellated here, ultimately flows into the problem of the union of the divine and the human spheres, of God and man, of spirit and world. I have the feeling that it is a claim on man which is directly connected with the development of the divine personality in the Old Testament. It would lead us too far to go more closely into this idea. But in any case, from this aspect of a divine demand it would again be justifiable to speak of a real tragedy in Saul's fate. Saul would thus be a victim of the divine idea of wholeness manifesting itself in him regardless, so to speak, of man and his human limits. It was impossible for Saul to fulfill this demand of wholeness. He was split by it. From this point of view he was, as it were, an attempt of the divine nature that failed. This would account for God's *repentance.* Even as a failure, however, he was still a witness of God's will, which although it was still chaotic was pregnant with meaning, as we can see in this just claim on man. It led on, as it were, into the future, where new possibilities could follow in the divine process of development.

Perhaps this idea also gives us a background from which we can understand the great honor which a Jewish legend pays to this unfortunate king in spite of his human guilt. In this legend God himself justifies Saul, so to speak, and once more lovingly accepts him in the order of his creative nature. I should like to bring this study to a close with a brief account of it:

A year after Saul and his sons had been killed, a famine came on the land for three successive years. And David sent out the people to find out whether there were any idolators in the land whose sin could be preventing rain, but nothing of the kind was found

In the second year he sent them out again and told them to search most diligently for any fornication in the land which might bring the drought as a punishment. But nothing of the kind was found.

Then David said: 'Now I know that it is I myself.' And he sought for the face of the Lord, and the Lord spake unto him: 'It is on account of Saul.' But David replied: 'Almighty ruler of the world! I am not Saul and there has been no idolatry in the land in my time. Moreover, I am not Saul who quarrelled with the prophet Samuel.'

Then David arose and gathered together the mighty and wise in Israel. They crossed the Jordan and came to Jabesh in Gilead. There they found the corpses of Saul and Jonathan, which no worm had gnawed. They put them into a shrine and returned across the Jordan, and buried them in the sepulchre of Saul's father, Kish, in the land of Benjamin, and they carried out all the king's commands. But what were the king's commands? The king had ordered them to take Saul's coffin throughout the whole land of Israel, into every region and into every village, and to take care that the people should everywhere pay due homage to the bodies. And it happened that all the people and their sons and daughters paid homage to the king's body and thus absolved their debt.

80

And when the Lord saw that the people had paid due honor to their king, he became compassionate and sent rain upon the land. [18]

oooooooooooooooooooooooooooooo

NOTES

1. Cf. also Gideon's vocation in Judges 6:15.
2. Tübingen, 1910.
3. It relates that David did penance for the sin he committed in connection with Bathsheba for twenty-two years, and was stricken with leprosy for six months. During all this time the Shekinah remained absent from him. (Talmud Tract, Joma 22b; quoted from *Encyclopaedia Judaica*, Article, "David", p. 828; see also Bin Gorion, *Sagen der Juden*, p. 620.)
4. Gesenius, *Hebräisches und Aramäisches Handwörterbuch*, s.v.
5. See Sellin, *Geschichte des Volkes Israel*, p. 147.
6. Cf. also I Chron. 17:13.
7. Cf. Jos. 10:11; I Sam. 7:10; I Sam. 14:15; II Kings 19:35, etc.
8. 1924, p. 11.
9. Ex. 17:16: For he (Moses) said, Because the Lord hath sworn that the Lord will have war with Amalek from generation to generation.
10. See Commentary on this passage in Nowack's *Handkommentar zum Alten Testament.*
11. See article, "Bann" in *Religion in Geschichte und Gegenwart.*
12. Cf. Lev. 17:21, 28, 29; Numbers 18:14; Deut. 7:2, 6; 13:17; Jos. 6:17, 18; 7:1ff.
13. Cf. also Chapter 14:32-35, where Saul appears as the stern guardian of ritual demand. He forbids his army to eat the meat with its blood. Cf. also in this connection Deut. 12:16-23 and Gen. 9:4.
14. Translated from *Die Bücher Samuelis*, 1902, p. 82.

15. Probably by a substitute. Cf. Budde, 1.c., p. 17.

16. See note to this passage in Kittel's *Biblia Hebraica.*

17. Micha Josef bin Gorion, *Die Sagen der Juden,* pp. 589-90. From *Midrash Leviticus Rabba,* 26, 7.

18. Bin Gorion, *Sagen der Juden,* pp. 593-94. From *Pirke de Rabbi Elieser,* Venice, 1544.

THE QUEEN OF SHEBA

IN BIBLE AND LEGENDS

PREFATORY NOTE

THE QUEEN OF SHEBA
IN BIBLE AND LEGENDS

"The Queen of Sheba in Bible and Legends"
was presented first as a lecture in honor of
C. G. Jung's 80th Birthday in July 1955. It was
later enlarged and given at the C. G. Jung Institute Zürich, in Los Angeles at the Analytical
Psychological Club (1967), at the C. G. Jung
Foundation in New York (1967), and in Basel
and San Francisco.

The translation was made by the author with the
kind collaboration of Yechezkel Kluger.

THE QUEEN OF SHEBA IN BIBLE AND LEGENDS

In I Kings 10, amid descriptions of King Solomon's wisdom and richness, we find the episode of his encounter with the Queen of Sheba. This episode seems to me to belong essentially in the line of religious development of Old Testament spirit and its *Auseinandersetzung* with the preceding pagan world; and it was not for nothing that this subject was amplified and developed further throughout the following centuries by a number of legends of great beauty and depth. I would like to present a small selection of this rich material. In making my choices it was my concern to give a survey of some main motifs which I thought to be the most interesting from the psychological point of view.

Let us turn first to the Old Testament text, which is the starting point and nucleus of the significant tissue of legends. It reads as follows:

> 1. And when the Queen of Sheba heard of the fame of Solomon concerning the name of the Lord, she came to prove him with hard questions.
> 2. And she came to Jerusalem with a very great train, with camels that bare spices, and very much gold, and precious stones: and when she was come to Solomon, she communed with him of all that was in her heart.
> 3. And Solomon told her all her questions: there was not any thing hid from the king, which he told her not.
> 4. And when the Queen of Sheba had seen all Solomon's wisdom, and the house that he had built,
> 5. And the meat of the table, and the sitting of his servants, and the attendance of his ministers, and their apparel, and his cupbearers, and his ascent by which he went up unto the house of the Lord; there was no more spirit in her.
> 6. And she said to the king, It was a true report that I heard in mine own land of thy acts and of thy wisdom.

7. Howbeit I believed not the words, until I came, and
mine eyes had seen it: and, behold, the half was not
told me: thy wisdom and prosperity exceedeth the
fame which I heard.
8. Happy are thy men, happy are these thy servants,
which stand continuously before thee, and that hear
thy wisdom.
9. Blessed be the Lord thy God, which delighted in
thee, to set thee on the throne of Israel: because the
Lord loved Israel for ever, therefore made he thee king,
to do judgment and justice.
10. And she gave the king an hundred and twenty talents
of gold, and of spices very great store, and precious
stones: there came no more such abundance of spices
as these which the Queen of Sheba gave to King Solomon.
. . .
13. And King Solomon gave the Queen of Sheba all her
desire, whatsoever she asked, beside that which Solomon
gave her of his royal bounty. So she turned and went
to her own country, she and her servants.

(I Kings 10:1-10, 13)

Before going into this text, I would like to give at least a glimpse
of the question of the Queen of Sheba's historicity. Pains have been
taken to find historical threads, but so far they have not enough
strength of proof. Most of the Old Testament passages when speaking
of the land of Sheba, among them our passage about the Queen of
Sheba herself, indicate, by their mention of the fabulous riches of the
land of Sheba — incense, spices, gold and precious stones — South
Arabia as her origin. The whole outfit of our queen places her into
this land of Sheba in Southern Arabia, which is approximately Yemen
of the present day, with the capital Marib. But so far there is no proof
of southern Arabia having been ruled at any time by queens. Lists of

Arabic rulers do include queens, but only in Hedjaz, in the north, not in the south. So far not only do we not know anything historically about queens in South Arabia, but we don't know anything about Sabean kings beyond about 800 B. C. (about 150-200 years after Solomon's time).[1] An American archaeological expedition led by Wendell Phillips entered Marib in 1952 but Yemen authorities prevented a complete exploration. Phillips describes the exciting adventures of this expedition in his book,[1a] which appeared in London in 1955. He sees "no reason to doubt that the queen was real." The proof, however, he leaves to future archaeological finds. He writes:

> Some day archaelogical research will confirm her exis-
> tence and tell us more about her, just as it has in recent
> years confirmed numerous other biblical stories of this
> same general period — for example, Solomon's chariot
> city uncovered during the excavations at Megiddo, his
> copper refineries recently revealed at Tel el-Kehleifeh,
> and the demonstrated expansion of the tenth century
> (B. C.) Phoenicians in the Mediterranean Sea.[2]

Taking it for granted that the Queen of Sheba lived in Marib, he has, however, to state that: "Nothing in that part of the world had previously gone back to her time, which was probably around 950 B. C."[3] and that "Actually, all we really know about the Queen of Sheba is found in the Bible."[4] That future excavations may bring to light proofs of the historical existence of the Queen of Sheba may or may not, of course, be so.

Phillips is overlooking one rather conspicuous and perhaps decisive fact, namely, that so far the only source for the Queen of Sheba, the biblical story in I Kings 10, is found in a highly legendary part of the biblical narrative of King Solomon. It is embedded in the description of his wisdom and his riches,[5] and it is also rather conspicuous, if the event described in I Kings 10 is taken as strictly historical, that the name of the visiting queen should not be mentioned. In this ardent insistence on the Queen's historicity, against which scientific soberness seems to have a difficult stand, one can feel a significant anima fascination.

The anima, the feminine soul image of man, goes back into antiquity and is sought in its remnants, into which she is projected. We may recall in this connection Rider Haggard's *She*,[6] where the search of the soul also leads the hero of the story into antiquity. And if the object of research is this mysterious Queen of Sheba with her unmistakable anima qualities, as it is my concern to show in the following, she is not the worst object a young American's anima projection could fall upon! Lest this be thought to be all my fantasy, I should like to quote the ending of Wendell Phillips' book, where he says, after having described the disappointing end of his archaeological expedition: "We can only dream of what our reception would have been like had our visit to Sheba's capital city taken place during the reign of Arabia's most famous queen. For she too was an explorer at heart."[7] At the same time, there is a deeper intuition hidden in Wendell Phillips' statement, for in the sense of inner search, the Queen of Sheba appears in the Bible and all the legends really as an "explorer at heart."

The powerful Queen seems to have exerted the same "real" fascination upon another scholar, namely Sir Ernest A. Wallis Budge, one of the main authorities on the history of Ethiopia, who writes, for instance: "As to the 'Queen of Sheba', it is very likely that some enterprising 'queen of the South' *did* make a journey to Jerusalem and interview Solomon...."[8] Equally, Budge, who throughout many passages of his book is very well aware of the historical problems and connections, states about the *Kebra Nagast*, the Ethiopean "Book of the Glory of the Kings," which contains the Ethiopean story of King Solomon as founder of the Ethiopean dynasty by his marriage with the Queen of Sheba: an inner psychological reality onto the outside, i.e., onto history, and to state about the *Kebra Nagast:*

88

"Many eminent scholars have accepted the story as historical, and I think on the whole they were right, and it is believed to this day by all classes in Abyssinia, who really regard Solomon as the first real king of their country..."[9] This shows the constellating power of an archetypal image, which, if not realized as such, is projected into outer historical reality.

The just mentioned *Kebra Nagast* contains the most elaborate saga about the Queen of Sheba; but in its given form it is nowadays rather unanimously considered as late, that is, not going back beyond the thirteenth century A. D. This version of the Queen of Sheba legend is obviously a Christian-Arabic loan, as seen, for instance, in the fact that Menelek is a corrupt form of Ibn-el-Hakim *(bnelhakim),* which means "Son of the Wise." [10] This is also indicated by the Christian elements in the *Kebra Nagast,* as, for instance, when the author quotes St. Paul and comments on the considerable polygamy of Solomon, saying that this has to do with the difference of the law in the Old and New Testaments, and that the Christians would not be able to keep up monogamy without participation in the body and blood of Christ. [11]

Another humorously naive anachronism may be mentioned here: one day, after having had the Queen of Sheba as his guest for six months, and after having met her for daily walks, he, coming from his palace and she, from hers, and having conversations with her, Solomon indulged in the following consideration: "Such a beautiful princess came to me from the end of the world. Who knows, whether God did not foresee for me posterity by her, as it is written in the Book of the Kings? [12] Deramey remarks about this passage: *"Il est vraiment dommage, que l'auteur n'ait pas cité le passage en question!"* [13]

Also the name of the Queen of Sheba in *Kebra Nagast*, Makeda, very likely goes back to the New Testament. It means "the Fiery One" and probably is a translation of the "Queen of the South" in Matthew

13:42. In Chapter 33 of the *Kebra Nagast,* the Queen of Sheba is identified with Queen Candace, mentioned as the "Queen of the Ethiopians" in the New Testament (Acts 8:27).

All these obvious signs of a late origin of the Ethiopian legend as it is found in the *Kebra Nagast,* and the great likelihood that it also was an expression of the understandable desire of a young dynasty to anchor itself way in the past (we just have to remember, for instance, the Babylonian list of the kings which goes back to the Gods), do not necessarily speak against the possibility that the legend may have been much older in Ethiopia itself, and may have been based on historical circumstances which account for its appearance in this country. It is interesting to note that in the *"Liber Axumae"* [14] (Axum was supposed to be the city where, according to the Ethiopian tradition, Makeda resided) great pains are taken to explain the name "Queen of Sheba"; i. e., to root it in the Ethiopian tradition. According to this, when Makeda came to the throne, she rebuilt the town in this territory of 'Aseba: It is for this reason that the Bible calls her "Queen of Saba," and also "Queen of 'Azēb" (i. e., South).[15] Another attempt to reconcile the discrepancy between Sheba and Ethiopia is to place Sheba at the western shore of the Red Sea, i.e., to identify it with Ethiopia. But the attempt of reconciliation itself indicates an underlying awareness of the fact that Sheba originally was not identical with Ethiopia. The legends mention a ship which King Solomon gives to the Queen at her departure, to make her come to him across the Red Sea. It was, by the way, not the only means of transportation she acquired from the generous king, since she received also "six thousand camels and wagons for traversing the desert..." [16] and, interesting in itself for appearing in a legend of the 13th century, a vessel "wherein one could traverse the air."[17] All these vehicles do not appear among Solomon's gifts as mentioned in the Old Testament. The real reason for the appearance of the Queen of Sheba in the Ethiopian tradition, though, may lie much more in a far earlier

historical and cultural connection of Yemen and Ethiopia. I follow
here Sir Ernest A. Wallis Budge, who says: "The facts of history
suggest that at the time when Solomon was reigning, about 970 B. C.,
the natives of the country which we now call Abyssinia were savages.
The Habasha tribe from Yaman were the first to introduce civilization
into the country... and the story of a queen who went to Jerusalem
probably entered the country with them."[18] He further states:
"The facts of history show that the Abyssinians borrowed everything
of importance from the nations round about them. Their oldest
civilization they owed to the Himyarites and Yamanites, and their
language is closely allied to that of the peoples in the south of the
Arabian Peninsula." [19]

This connection between Sheba and Ethiopia, through the influx
of Sabean folklore into Ethiopia, might very well have already been
traditional knowledge in the lifetime of the historian Flavious Josephus
(first century, A. D.), which may underlie his identification of Sheba
with Ethiopia: he speaks of the Queen of Sheba as the Queen of
Egypt and Ethiopia. [20]

Apart from the legendary character of our biblical story there is
another track leading us in the same direction: in Arabic folklore the
Queen of Sheba's name is *Bilqis* or *Balqis*. There are many legends
around Bilqis and she seems to have been a popular figure in Arabic
folklore even before the Islamic time. It thus seems very likely that
Bilqis is the name of a legendary Arabic queen, who has been identified
with the Queen of Sheba in Islamic times, when the biblical and later
Jewish legends had been taken over. [21] There is, furthermore, a theory
presented in literature that the name Bilqis or Balqis is a phonetic transformation of the Himyaritic (i. e., South Arabic name of the God *Ilmukah*
or *Ilumkuh*[22]),which seems to hint at an original identity of this God
with Bilqis.[23] At any rate, this theory seems to be supported by the
fact that one of the temples of Ilmuqah, who is a moon god, is still now-

adays called by the native population "Haram Bilqis," [24] which means:
the harem, or the women's house of Bilqis. [25] This indicates an ancient
connection between Queen Bilqis and the South Arabian religion.

Identification of the moon god Ilmuqah and Queen Bilqis allows a
further conclusion: namely, that she at least came close to the status
of a goddess. This is also strongly supported by the fact that the name
Almaquh appears alone or in connection with Athtar, who, though masculine, is one with Ishtar (Venus).[26]

Furthermore, we must in this connection consider that Sheba was
the land of magicians, par excellence, in which occult arts and astrology
were especially cultivated.[27]

With all this in view, and bearing in mind the fact that up till now
there has been no historical indication of the Queen of Sheba, it seems
to me that, considering the highly legendary, and even mythological,
character of most of the stories about her, we cannot go wrong if we
leave the Queen of Sheba in her mystery and the legends woven around it.

From all that we know about her, she appears, as it were, the
royal symbol of the feminine genius of Arabia Felix, and, in our biblical
account especially, as a messenger from the remote land of origin, the
unconscious. It seems to me this is also suggested by the very atmosphere of the biblical story itself, and it is confirmed by its later ampli-
fication in the Jewish and Arabic legends. And let us not forget that the
Queen of Sheba's biblical partner, King Solomon, in spite of, or beyond,
his important historical existence, became *the* Jewish legendary king
par excellence. The beginning of this development we find in the Bible
itself, especially in I Kings, 4:29-34, [28] where we read:

> And God gave Solomon wisdom and understanding exceed-
> ing much, and largeness of heart, even as the sand that is on

the sea shore.
And Solomon's wisdom excelled the wisdom of all the children of the east country, and all the wisdom of Egypt.
For he was wiser than all men;...and his fame was in all
nations round about.

...

And he spake of trees, from the cedar tree that is in Lebanon
even unto the hyssop that springeth out of the wall: he
spake also of beasts, and of fowl, and of creeping things,
and of fishes.
And there came of all peoples to hear the wisdom of Solomon,
from all kings of the earth, which had heard of his wisdom.

The sentence: "He spake also of beasts *('al)*, and of fowl and of creeping things and of fishes," was later interpreted as "he spoke *to ('el)*" all
these creatures. [29] In the legends it has always been understood this
way. There he not only understood the language of the birds and other
animals, but he also ruled over a tremendous army of demons, with
whose help he even built the temple. He is the Jewish king, the chosen
one of Yahweh. But at the same time, he carries unmistakable features
of a sorcerer, a fact which shows itself in our connection to be of greatest significance. One could say that he is the builder of the temple of
Yahweh, but, at the same time, the whole pagan background is still alive
in him, the pagan anima, so to speak. This could be seen as a symbolic
anticipation of a future development, of a union of the opposites. It
throws light onto certain Jewish legends, in which Solomon achieves the
significance of an anthropos figure, and in which he is given the dignity
of an almost divine rank. In *Midrash Bereshith Rabba,* for instance, we
read: "The power over the animal world, lost by Adam through his sin,
was regained by Solomon." [30] And in the *Talmud:* "Solomon before
his fall was lord over all the terrestrials and celestials..." [31] The church
fathers turned against these statements in the legends, maintaining that
scriptural passages speaking of man's dominion over the entire creation

can only refer to Jesus. [32] Also, an Arabic legend of the birth of Solomon reminds one of a Messiah birth: The child Solomon is born with a radiance of light in his face; Iblis (i.e., Satan) and his hosts melt as lead or iron melts in fire; the angels come down on earth to assist at the birth; the earth is laughing in joy; the wild animals bow towards him and the tame ones come near. [33]

As a human being, however, King Solomon was not up to the inner constellation of the pagan anima at all: he succumbed to her by marrying the Egyptian princess, who pulled him into a regression, i. e., into pagan cults and material culture. His realm went to pieces through his love of luxury, and he died an effeminate Oriental despot. So it is not mere chance that in a legend this Egyptian princess appears as identical with the Queen of Sheba. But it is significant precisely in our connection, for in the biblical text there is no marriage between King Solomon and the Queen of Sheba.

> And when the Queen of Sheba heard of the fame of Solomon concerning the name of the Lord, she came to prove him with hard questions.

(I Kings 10:1)

The Hebrew word *nasā* means actually "to test," and also, "to tempt." And *ḥidōt* not only means "hard questions," but "riddles"; i.e., she came to tempt (test) him with riddles. The riddles themselves are not mentioned in the biblical text. There it only says:

> And Solomon told her all her questions: there was not anything hid from the king, which he told her not.

(I Kings 10:3)

Some commentators see here only a harmless royal game of society,

94

comparable to oriental riddle tournaments and those known from the courts of the Middle Ages. But, as André Chastel points out, the riddle tournament is really a mirroring of a *struggle for power.* Presenting a riddle to someone which he cannot answer [34] is a certain way of taking possession over him. Going a little further along this line, we could add that, by admitting to not knowing, a person submits to the greater power of knowledge of the asking one. The Queen of Sheba provokes King Solomon with her questions; behind this, we sense a matter of competition between the two magicians, which is of decisive importance. It seems that we are concerned here with a faded, but nevertheless significant, Sphinx background: not only is the nature of the questions, which the legends filled in, somewhat similar to that of the Sphinx riddles (questions which look complicated but point to basic facts of life), but the very fact that the Queen of Sheba questions Solomon has the character of a test. She came, as the biblical text says, "to prove him with hard questions." The implication from the archetypal pattern of such questioning is that the defeated one has to pay, to give up some possession which can range from some object to life itself. There are many examples of riddles having been a matter of life and death. [35] The only other Old Testament story in which the riddle test occurs is the story of Samson in Judges 14: the riddle game, started as a wedding entertainment, leads up to the macabre ending of the Samson story, in which the Philistine wife of Samson, by extracting from him the secret of his power, and thus breaking it, acts as the negative anima, inducing the tragedy.

J. A. Kelso, in his article, "Riddle," in Hasting's *Religion and Ethics,* [36] presents several other interesting examples of the riddle as a matter of life and death, of which I would like to mention a few. Plutarch supports the legend of a struggle of this type between Theognis and Homer, in which the latter is defeated and dies of mortification. In a very close parallel to the Sphinx riddle are some modern Greek legends, in which the failure to solve a riddle costs a man his life. A monster living in a castle propounds a riddle and gives forty days for its solution. Unfortunate is the person who fails, for the monster devours him. In the Teutonic legend of the Wartburg Krieg, there is a deadly riddle contest between Odin and the giant Wafthrudhuir. In the *Mahabharata*, the decisive importance of the riddle for life and death is seen in another way: the hero Yudhishtira frees two brothers from the fetters of a monster by the solution of a riddle. The same pattern as the Sphinx story itself appears in the legend of the Chinese princess Turandot, which became famous by Schiller's drama of this name, which had a Persian source;[37] and it also is contained in *The Arabian Nights*. Turandot agrees to marry only the prince who can solve her riddles: the others who try to woo her under this fatal condition, and fail, are heartlessly beheaded and their heads are planted on the poles of the fence before the palace. Incidentally, it is one of the weaker dramas of this genius. There is nothing to be felt of the archetypal background of the story and its inherent psychological meaning.[38] It remains absolutely incomprehensible why this fury of a princess suddenly changes into a loving wife at the end after all. There is an interesting intuitive beginning: Turandot hates men, because they only want her for her beauty; they don't want *her,* they are just possessively greedy. But so is the noble prince Kalaf: he becomes a victim of a spell-like infatuation upon seeing her picture; no reason for his deadly struggle is given, other than to possess this beauty. It becomes even more astonishing that he continues to "love" this monster. The deeper tones of an underlying pattern of the redemption of an animus-possessed woman, to which the legend would easily have lent itself, are lacking in Schiller's drama.

A deeper grasp of this subject we find in Pierre Benoit's *Atlantide,* in which the image of the cruel Antinéa is filled and enlarged to represent the negative anima in all her aspects. She combines the beauty of Venus, the cleverness of the serpent and the gruesomeness of a wild beast. She fascinates all men who come close to her, and perish through their love of her. As in the story of Turandot, Antinéa's lovers also are used as trophies. Their mummified corpses in statue form are placed as decorations in a mausoleum made for this purpose. And similar to Turandot, Antinéa acts (according to her own explanation) out of revenge against man, who misused woman through centuries surely and did not give her adequate evaluation.[39]

Certain relics from the times when the unsuccessful competitor actually lost his life are still to be found (according to Kelso in the article mentioned above) in certain parts of Germany, where the boy who fails to solve a riddle is greeted with such expressions as: "Er ist des Henkers" (he is the hangman's); "Muss sich zum Henker scheren" (has to go to the hangman); "Kommt in die Hölle" (goes to hell); or "Ist tot" (is dead). [40]

These examples and the only other riddle story in the Old Testament are apt to support the feeling of a faded, uncanny Sphinx background for our Queen of Sheba story. In the Sphinx story itself, as you know, it is, from the very beginning, a question of life and death to solve the riddle. Had Oedipus not solved it, he would have been killed by her.[41] And the Sphinx, being overcome by Oedipus' answer, confirms her defeat dramatically by jumping into the abyss. Oedipus overcomes the Sphinx, but falls into incest with Iocaste. The victory over the Sphinx is the beginning of the heroic conquest of the Great Mother, but the tragic feature of Oedipus' inability to pursue the heroic way is inherent in the oracle, which leads him into the fateful mother-incest and subsequent disaster. There is, however, a development in the happenings: one might say that the most inhuman aspect of the Great Mother died in the suicide of the Sphinx, whilst Iocaste is a human being with some insight and conscience, who commits suicide when she learns of her unconscious incest with her son. But under the tragic spell of the oracle, she remains for Oedipus on the line of the negative, devouring mother, of which the Sphinx is the most inhuman, archaic form.

The Sphinx has a truly horrid background: she is a daughter of
Echidna, who in her upper part is a beautiful virgin, in her lower, a
snake; Echidna is the daughter of Gaia, the earth mother, and Tartaros,
the underworld personified; Gorgo, Cerberus and a row of dragons are
her daughters and sons; and the Sphinx she begat with one of her sons,
Orthrus, the dog of the terrible Geryon. So the Sphinx is an impressive personification of the devouring mother; she is the riddle of nature
itself, in its devouring aspect. The content of her riddle is a hint to
nature-bound human existence; its answer amounts to a conscious *ac-
knowledgement of the way of nature.* This might explain the suicide
of the Sphinx: after her riddle is answered, she loses her power in the
aspect of the blindest inhuman nature. An author of the last century,
J. B. Friedreich, writes in his *Geschichte des Rätsels* on the question of
the Sphinx's suicide: "If a riddle is solved, it ceases to be a riddle, it is
killed as such." [42] In answering the Sphinx's riddle, Oedipus has overcome the devouring aspect of the Mother Archetype in its crudest archaic form. The hero is the one who solves the problem of the time.
Had Oedipus not taken the challenge of the Sphinx, Thebes, the city,
would not have been released. The city is a symbol of human culture
and consciousness born out of the *prima materia* of the unconscious.
The heroic deed to save it has been performed by Oedipus. But one decisive element of the hero myth is lacking in the Oedipus myth: he cannot yet free himself, as we have seen, into a new consciousness. He remains in his own fate a victim of the oracle, of the Great Mother
as blind cruel nature.

It is another Greek hero, Odysseus, who can be looked upon as being
closer to stepping out of the spell of the Great Mother: For he refuses to
give the blood, his vitality, to the shadow of his mother in the underworld,
and he is up to the devouring charms of Circe. He has a counter-charm
with him, the herb Moly, given to him by Hermes, and a sword, a symbol of

discrimination.[43] In Perseus' killing of the Gorgo (a sister of Echidna), the intellect, symbolized in the reflecting mirror and the sickle with which he kills her, plays the decisive role. The sickle points to the primeval mother Gaia, who had her son, Kronos, dismember her husband, Uranos, with the sickle she had fashioned. In Perseus' deed, the sickle turns against her and kills her. Out of Gorgo's terrifying head, the winged horse Pegasus is freed, uniting, as a symbol, instinct and spirit;[44] also a giant, symbol of the hero's masculine strength, is freed from the devouring mother. The release of the anima, Andromeda, who, tied to a rock, was in the power of a sea monster (another form of the devouring mother), is a further step of the hero myth: the hero, freed from the mother, frees his own soul.[45]

This is a step not yet reached in the earlier Near Eastern hero myths. But in the Near Eastern myths, as in the Gilgamesh epic and the Marduk myth, there is also a breakthrough into new spiritual development and creativity. This is seen in the Gilgamesh epic in the birth of a new search for individual immortality, and in the Marduk myth in a new discriminative creativity: Marduk creates heaven and earth out of the body of the defeated devouring mother. In any case, the overcoming of the negative aspect of the Great Mother is accomplished in all these myths by symbols of discriminative spiritual functioning. Also, Gilgamesh's refusal of Ishtar's proposal fits the pattern: his words function as a mirror in which she might have reflected herself, if she could have! But she is seen through; her riddle is solved, which explains Gilgamesh's attitude as having the effect of a defeat; after which, she curses Gilgamesh and mourns her broken power.[46] This is a clear parallel to the more drastic suicide of the Sphinx. So we can say that the Sphinx riddle has to be solved, as an act of awareness of the essence of nature. If one is not aware of it, one succumbs to its destructive aspect. Gilgamesh, who overcame Ishtar, is confronted with the problem of death; and with the wisdom which he brings home from the inner night sea journey, he must accept the reality of human limitations, without succumbing again to the unconscious in its negative aspect. Similarly, after his inner journey Odysseus comes home to his hearth and family, in the order of human nature, indicating wholeness.

In his book, *Das Rätsel der Sphinx, Grundzüge einer Mythengeschichte*, [47] Ludwig Laistner gives a very interesting modern folklore example of a Sphinx-like demon of noon. He writes:

> The Wends know of the mid-day woman (Pripolniza), a tall figure in white garments, who appeared at noontime between twelve and two o'clock in the fields, and stood unexpectedly before those who had failed to interrupt their work in the fields at noon and to go home. The surprised people had to go through a difficult examination on the cultivation of flax and the weaving of linen, and to talk so elaborately that all the time until two o'clock was filled. When the bell rang two o'clock, *the power of the mid-day woman ceased and she left.* But if the frightened people did not know how to answer the questions, and were not able to keep up the talk until the bell rang, she cut their heads off with the sickle, which she carried with her, or she strangled them or at least gave them an illness connected with terrible headaches. [48]

Again, we see in this story that the Sphinx-like question was concerned with facts of nature: the cultivation of flax and the weaving of linen. Interestingly enough, in the Second Targum to The Book of Esther, [49] there is a riddle put to King Solomon by the Queen of Sheba that also points to the flax. It runs as follows:

> A piper passes over its head and it utters a loud and bitter cry, its head is like a reed, it is honor for the rich, disgrace for the poor, honor for the dead, disgrace for the living, joy to birds, trouble for fishes. The answer is *flax,* because the wind pipes over the flax stalks, linen furnishes garments of varying value to different classes of men, from flax are made shelters for birds, nets for fishes. [50]

The fact that those people who fail to make a break at noon, and work on, are questioned by the mid-day woman, seems to point to the necessity of interruption, of stepping out of the identity with nature, of reflecting on it, so to speak; otherwise they are forced to do so in a negative way; they are forced to solve the riddles of nature. If they can solve them, the mid-day demon disappears, i.e., she is overcome; if not, she becomes the man-killing Sphinx.

This story is unique in that it unites the Sphinx motif with two other archetypal manifestations of the negative mother: The sickle she uses traces her back to the primeval mother, Gaia,[51] and behind the strangling mid-day demon, Lilith appears, the demonic first wife of Adam, who goes after newborn children, strangling them at night. We will see that this is not the only association with Lilith. The headaches can be looked upon as an expression of the tension caused by the unsolved riddle. It happens not infrequently that headaches appear before a breakthrough of some sort. They even appear in myths, as for instance with Zeus, who, we are told, had a terrible headache before Pallas Athene was born out of his head.

In a parallel saga of the Spreewald, a woman decided to stay over noon in the field and to talk a full hour with the Pshesponiza about flax, and did so until twelve o'clock, at which moment the time of the Pshesponiza was up. The Pshesponiza had to leave and never came again.

In another version the Pshesponiza says: "Now you have taken my power away, now I am free, and you too are free." But then she adds enigmatically, "Another time don't dare do that again!" There seems to be no "once for ever" in the psychological process of becoming conscious; the unconscious can put us before the same task more than once. And yet, the Pshesponiza declares herself to be not only overcome, but *free*. She is redeemed, for she was under a spell.

In a variation of the Niederlausitz, she says even before leaving: "So,

101

now I am redeemed." And also here, as in the Spreewald version, she didn't appear again in that field. Here a new and most interesting element enters our investigation. These folkloristic stories don't mention what the cause of the spell was, nor into what the Sphinx-like mid-day woman was changed after her redemption. But we are presented with a problem of redemption of the Sphinx, for which more elaborate sagas will offer us an answer.[52]

Let us return to the Queen of Sheba: As has been pointed out, this whole uncanny background has faded in our biblical story; also in the legends, the right answer to the questions is no longer a matter of life and death. But in the emphasis laid on the right answers given by King Solomon we can still feel the power struggle in the background. For power, the right answer is decisive. The Queen of Sheba is wise, but King Solomon proves himself to be still wiser, or at least to be also in possession of her wisdom. But instead of a disappearance on the part of the loser, according to the usual pattern, something decisively new happens: the Queen of Sheba *bows* before King Solomon as the stronger one, saying:

> ...It was a true report that I heard in mine own land of thy acts and of thy wisdom.
> Howbeit I believed not the words, until I came, and mine eyes had seen it: and, behold, the half was not told me: thy wisdom and prosperity exceedeth the fame which I heard.

> (I Kings 10:6,7)

But this is not enough. The whole happening does not remain on the level of a power struggle, where only victory and defeat exist. Not only does the Queen of Sheba in our biblical story seem not to have any negative feelings about her defeat, to say nothing of the fact that she does not throw herself into the abyss like the defeated Sphinx, but in her defeat she seems to change. She seems to have a longing for something higher, a longing for a wisdom which transcends hers, for she says: "Happy are thy women, happy are thy servants, which stand continually before thee, and that hear thy wisdom." (I Kings 10:8). You will find in the English translation: "Happy are thy men..." But the Zürich Bible translates according to Septuaginta, Latina and Syriaca, "women," reading *nāšim* instead of *'anašim* (men). It makes more sense that the Queen of Sheba should envy the *women* around Solomon who live in the aura of his wisdom.

Like Solomon's women, like his servants, she would like to always be close to him in order to participate in his wisdom. It can already here in the biblical story be surmised, as will become obvious in the later legends, that it was this very longing that actually put her on her way. For in the verses which immediately follow, her submission deepens into a full acceptance of a new religious content. She says:

> Blessed be the Lord thy God, which delighted in thee, to
> set thee on the throne of Israel: because the Lord loved
> Israel for ever, therefore made he thee king, to do judg-
> ment and justice.

(I Kings 10:9)

In the Koran, what is here only hinted at developed into a story of conversion: the Queen of Sheba converts to Islam. But already in our biblical text it becomes clear that it is a matter of an encounter of the Queen of the South, as a representative of the Sabaean paganism, with the Hebrew King Solomon. [53]

But how does our story end? The Queen of Sheba presents King Solomon with rich gifts, as we have seen. There follows in the text then an insertion about the treasures of King Hiram, which were brought to King Solomon from the gold land of Ophir; then the text

103

goes on:

> And king Solomon gave unto the queen of Sheba all her
> desire, whatsoever she asked, beside that which Solomon
> gave her of his royal bounty. So she turned and went
> to her own country, she and her servants.

(I Kings 10:13)

From the point of view of the symbolic background of the happening,
i.e., the encounter of the pagan Queen with the monotheistic King, one
would expect the royal *coniunctio* to be the lysis. After the exchange
of gifts, of values, the pagan Queen leaves, expressing the longing in her
heart. She would like to be one of the women and servants of the King,
who are always able to be around him and listen to his wisdom. What
happens to her longing? And what to King Solomon, having touched
her inner ground by solving her riddles? One gets the feeling that something remains suspended in this separation. I think that this has to do
with the problem of the time. It is as if the *coniunctio* could not yet
take place, because the danger of a mere regression into nature is yet
too great. One only has to think of the continuous struggle the prophets carried out against this ever present danger of backsliding into polytheistic cults. The spiritual side of the King was not yet ready to really
integrate the pagan anima, although the latter was longing for it. An
established masculinity is required for meeting the anima without falling
victim to her; the riddle solving is not enough. In reality, Solomon did
fall into being her victim, as we have seen from the historical facts of his
life. [54]

But just as we sensed the power of the Sphinx in the Queen of Sheba's
questioning of Solomon, so also is there the power of nature's riches in
her gifts. There is a subtle difference in the text's mention of her gifts
and those of Solomon. Hers are detailed:

104

And she gave the king an hundred and twenty talents of
gold, and of spices very great store, and precious stones:
there came no more such abundance of spices as these
the queen of Sheba gave to king Solomon.

(I Kings 10:10)

However this enumeration is lacking when it comes to the King's gifts.
In a mysterious generality, the text says:

And king Solomon gave unto the queen of Sheba all her
desire, whatsoever she asked, beside that which Solomon
gave her of his royal bounty

(I Kings 10:13)

The Hebrew text literally says: "beside that which Solomon gave her
according to the hand of the King Solomon."

Concerning the enumeration of the Queen of Sheba's gifts, one is
reminded of the gifts the Mother Goddess, Ishtar, promises to Gilgamesh
when wooing him to be her lover. It was a matter of life and death for
Gilgamesh to refuse them. He is the hero of a myth showing the transition from the era of the powerful Mother Goddess to a new spiritual path,
an early dawn of a new light, a new consciousness, leading to the Judaeo-
Christian spiritual development. After Gilgamesh rejected Ishtar's
proposal and her gifts, she raged in the form of a heavenly bull against
the dawning masculine world. But seen from this primeval background
of development, looking at the process, so to speak, from the other
end, we notice not only the lacking *coniunctio*, but also something
highly significant in the symbolic encounter between the Queen of and
King Solomon. It is something which hints toward the future, a mutual
approach of spirit and nature which aims toward a future redeeming
union. It looks like an anticipation of a later development, a lysis of
that tragic break of the marriage between Elohim (God) and Eden

105

in a gnostic myth, [55] in which nature remained below and became
evil, while the spirit withdrew to above and left nature alone.

The biblical account of the encounter of the Queen of Sheba with
King Solomon is only *a promise* for the healing of the breach. In the
Queen's *longing* and the King's *yielding* ("he gave her all her desire,
whatsoever she asked") lies a *promise for a future development.* But
only legends in post-biblical time bring the fulfillment, most elaborately
in the Ethiopian legend which will occupy us in detail, that of the union
of the royal couple being the origin of the Abyssinian dynasty. Although
here the symbolic happening is projected into history, while keeping its
religious numinosity, it was the privilege of a much later time to produce the spiritual blossom of the *coniunctio* between the Queen of
Sheba and King Solomon in its deepest form, namely in alchemy, as
we will see.

First the development went on, however, in another direction: the
Queen of Sheba appeared in many legends in her dark aspect. It is as if,
by going back to her country in the biblical account, she had again been
repressed into the unconscious and thereby *demonized.* In a demonized
form, or at least with demonic attributes which are more obvious even
than the conspicuous questions in the biblical story, she appears in these
legends before King Solomon; even in an older version of the Ethiopian
legend, this leads up to the *coniunctio* of King and Queen. It is as if the
full realization of her demonic character, which is already hinted at by
her Sphinx background in the biblical narrative, is necessary in order
that her *need for redemption,* which revealed itself in her desire to be
able to always be around Solomon, could come into full light. Her demonic side and her redemption from it appear, as a matter of fact, in
so many Jewish and Arabic legends that the motif of the *redemption
of the Sphinx,* which we previously met in some European folktales, [56]
becomes most obvious.

106

From what we have seen up to now, we could say that this motif would belong to a phase of the process of *Auseinandersetzung,* coming to terms, between nature and spirit, feminine and masculine, where the mere nature power is partially broken in having its riddle solved, its essence recognized. This being recognized, or "known," taken as an act of essential comprehension, brings up the longing in the feminine for the "knowing" one, for spirit. The redemption of the Sphinx thus becomes the task of man, of that masculine spirit which did *not* fall victim to her. In man's not falling her victim, the Sphinx can be redeemed of her mere matter (mater) aspect, to which her own primitive demonic spirit belongs, her power animus. It is the spiritual in man which redeems his anima out of mere nature, and correspondingly, the positive animus in woman which develops her femininity. The redemption of the Sphinx, seen from masculine psychic development, is really a next step in the archetypal pattern of overcoming the mother, the central subject of Jung's *Symbols of Transformation.* The challenge of the Sphinx is indeed just a specific form of that threatening challenge of the archetypal Great Mother, which Jung says "can become the source of energy for an heroic conflict; indeed, so obvious is this impression that one has to ask oneself whether the apparent enmity of the mother archetype is not a ruse on the part of Mater Natura for spurring on her favorite child to his highest acheivement." [57]

But as mentioned before, our special motif deals with the other side, so to speak; namely, with what the heroic deed of defeating the Sphinx, and therewith overcoming her, does to *her.* The range of reaction goes from the archaic destructive temper of Ishtar or the suicide of the Greek Sphinx, to the Queen of Sheba's inner submission to that Spirit which solved her riddle, in our biblical story. Her conversion to Islam in the Koran version of the legend, or to the God of Israel in the *Kebra Nagast,* the Ethiopian version, is a clear symbol of this inner change. But on top of that, the redemption in almost all of the versions is symbolized in the, above-mentioned, freeing by King Solomon of the Queen of Sheba from her demonic stigma.

I would especially like to present you with some legends in which this motif of the *redemption of the anima* as mere nature is expressed not only in the riddles and their solution, but also through the fact that the Queen of Sheba is freed by King Solomon from her demonic stigma. While in the first Jewish legend the anima aspect of the Queen of Sheba is more in the foreground, two Abyssinian legends show more of the feminine animus aspect of the process. By comparing the two legendary complexes, we have the rare opportunity to observe the same process, so to speak, from the masculine as well as the feminine angle. And thereby it becomes clear how much masculine anima development and feminine animus development are corresponding processes.

Let us look first at the Jewish legend: It is especially known in the form in which we find it in the 27th Sura of the Koran. But there it is obviously incomplete; there are gaps in the connection of events, which become understandable only through the knowledge of former texts. Very likely, Muhammed took this story over. as he did so many others, from the Jewish legend; later, the commentators of the Koran enriched the legend, partly from the Jewish model and partly out of their own rich fantasy. Most likely, the Koran version goes back to the so-called Second Targum to the Book of Esther, which is not old as such, but uses old sources.[58] Both texts show several literal correspondences.

Here is how the story in the Second Targum to the Book of Esther goes:

> When Solomon's heart was merry with wine, he commanded
> the beasts of the field and the birds of the sky and the spirits
> and demons to be brought before him. One day the hoopoe
> was missing among the birds and he could not be found. The
> King became very angry about him, but finally calmed down
> again, when the hoopoe arrived and told him the reason for
> his absence: he had, he told the King, flown all over the world,
> in order to find out: 'Is there a country or a kingdom, which
> is not subject to my Lord the King? ' And thus it happened

that he found the town Kitor, in the country of the *rising sun*. 'The land is full of *gold and silver*,' the hoopoe reports, 'the *trees there are standing from the creation, and they are watered from the Garden of Eden.* Many peoples are there, on their heads they have *crowns* from *the Garden of Eden.* They know nothing of warfare, nor can they draw the bow. But I saw there also a woman, who rules over them all, and Queen of Sheba (Malkath Sheba) is her name.' [59]

We see that *a bird, an intuitive thought* of the King, has discovered the paradisiac realm of the unconscious under the government of the anima, and the libido of the King is immediately drawn to it, as we will see from the continuation.

You will have asked yourself, too, whether the type of bird is of any symbolic meaning, for which the legend itself might give a key. It should first be said that there are other birds mentioned in some legends, cock of the wood, and especially, lapwing or peewit, which in the dictionaries are identical, and of which the Winston Dictionary says: "Any of several Old World ploverlike birds, especially one species *(vanellus vanellus)* called peewit." Both the peewit and the hoopoe are characterized by a long slender bill; the latter, in addition, has, according to Winston's Dictionary, an erectile tuft of feathers on his head. (In German the lapwing or peewit is the *Kiebitz*, the hoopoe the *Wiedehopf*.) For both kinds we have some indicative statements in the legends themselves. In an Arabic version, we read:

As Solomon was returning on the carpet from Mecca, a
ray of sunlight penetrated through the bird canopy over-
head, and smote him. By this he knew that one of the
birds was absent from its post. So he summoned the
eagle, and bade him call each of the birds by name, so
to find which of them was missing. The eagle returned
with the news that the peewit was absent. Solomon

109

was greatly displeased at this, *for the peewit was indis-*
pensable because it could detect water even in a desert
or at the greatest depth. [60]

So this is the function of this bird: to find the water, the source of life,
in the desert, or at the greatest depth of the unconscious.

In another Arabian story, [61] however, the hoopoe left the bird canopy
over King Solomon's head because he was deliberately striking on the
day of the King's marriage as a result of the King's request for the feath-
ered slaves to pay the same honor to his bride as to himself. But the
King, missing his favorite bird, ordered the others to go and find the hoopoe. He was discovered after many months, crouching in a hole in the
rock on an island in the most distant of the seven seas. Upon being
found, seeing that he could not escape, he said: "I go with you against
my will to Suleyman, whose folly in asking us to do homage to the
most worthless of creatures exasperates and disgusts me." Then follow
three stories about the worthlessness and untrustworthiness of women,
and the necessity of keeping them short and under control. "You see
from these true stories," concluded the hoopoe, "what silly, vain and
tiresome creatures women are, and how wrong it was of Suleyman to
ask us to do homage to one of them..." The assembled birds acquiesced
in the soundness of the hoopoe's remarks. They considered that, if
these valuable facts were known to Suleyman, he would change his ways
with women and perhaps reward the hoopoe for having dared, from such
humane motives, to disobey him. They all returned to the King, who,
when he had listened to the hoopoe's three stories, took *the crown off*
his head and placed it on that of the bird, whose descendants wear it
to this day. So the hoopoe's crown is nothing less than the personal
one of King Solomon, who was grateful to this bird for good advice in
the direction of "taming the shrew." The author gives the interesting
information that, for this reason, the hoopoe is called still today by the

fellahin (the Arab peasants) "the wise man's bird," or "the bird of Suleyman el Hakim." [62]

If we look a little closer with psychological eyes, this bird could represent on the subjective level, seen from the person of King Solomon,
an inner knowledge which compensates the proverbial anima drivenness
of this King. The bird, the King's own wise intuition, rebels against his
tendency to follow every whim of the inhabitants of his harem and
to succumb to their plots. The bird's role in this primitive, folkloristic story fits, nevertheless, into the more subtle depth of our story,
where the bird is *the mediator to the anima,* whom he wants to see as
submissive to his King. And while King Solomon is not up to his women
in reality, he is, in the biblical story, up to the Queen of Sheba, who appeared out of the unconscious. Let us now go on with our legend:

As soon as the hoopoe finished his report about the marvelous country
he found, and its Queen, he offered the King to gird up his loins like a
mighty man, and to go to the city of Kitor, in the land of Sheba, to bring
their kings and nobles to Solomon, by force, if necessary. "And this
saying pleased Solomon," the text goes on. All the royal scribes were
called and a letter to the Queen of Sheba was written and tied to the wing
of the hoopoe, "who thereupon lifted up his wings, and soared up in the
air, and the other birds all followed him. And they came to the city of
Kitor in the land of Sheba. And it was in the morning time, and the
Queen had gone out to *worship the sun.* Suddenly the *multitude of ap-
proaching birds obscured the sunlight, and the Queen lifted her hand and
rent her garment into pieces and was mightily astonished.*"

Here we learn something highly significant about the Queen of Sheba:
She is a worshipper of the sun; she already is turned towards consciousness. The birds, messengers of a spiritual origin unconscious to her, obscure her sun. Her awestricken gesture at this numinous occurrence, i.e.,
tearing her garment, looked at symbolically points to a change of attitude

111

which presupposes the sacrifice of the old one. King Solomon's birds obscure her sun; something new is in preparation. She then discovers the letter tied to the wing of the hoopoe, who had flown down to her. She reads it and thereupon falls into new astonishment and fear: for the letter contains an invitation, which if rejected threatens death. From the point of view of the individuation process this means nothing less than that she *must* follow. If women don't follow such a call out of the unconscious, it *is* a kind of psychological death, in view of the inner goal of wholeness, because it amounts to declining spiritual development.

Now something very interesting happens: her elders and princes did not want to enter into this matter. "We do not know Solomon, nor do we esteem his kingdom," they say. And the text reports: *"But she put no confidence in them, nor listened to their words."* [63] Thus she literally turned away from the old spirit, her old animus court, and turned to a new unknown one. She sent a great delegation equipped with wonderful treasures to King Solomon, and gave them a letter, in which she had written these words: "From the city of Kitor to the land of Israel is in truth a journey of seven years, *but because of the questions which I desire to ask thee I shall come in three years*." Another version of the story renders it: "But since it is thy wish and thy desire, that I shall visit you, I will come already after three years." [64] I think the second version just keeps up her persona more, for it is more likely her own inner truth that hurries her. And so it happened; she appeared before King Solomon after a journey of three years.

The deeper meaning of this surprising readiness, we may even speak of a yearning drivenness, reveals itself soon in an unexpected way: For it happens that the Queen, in her encounter with King Solomon, got cornered in her *unconscious demonic* quality. King Solomon, so it says, had heard from the Djinns, his demons, that the Queen of Sheba was a *demon.* In a fragmentary Coptic version, it was the jealous wives of Solomon who made this insinuation. [65] And this he tested: He ordered the

Djinns to build a place with a glass floor, and there he received the Queen of Sheba: "And when the Queen of Sheba saw the King, she thought in her heart, that he sat in the water, and she lifted her garments, in order to cross the water, and so he saw, that she had hairy legs." With some Arabic authors this is exaggerated to the statement that her whole body was covered with hair, and with Ta'alabi and another Koran commentator, Dschelaleddin al Mahalli, [66] it is even a matter of her having the feet of an ass. With Ta'alabi, this is outspokenly a sign of *demonic origin*. The feet of an ass remind us of the Arabic ghul, and these again of Lilith. The *se'irim* in the Bible, desert demons appearing in Isaiah 34, live with Lilith in the ruins of the desert; the significance of their name means nothing else but "the hairy ones." [67] This feature is not the only one linking Balqis, as the Queen of Sheba is called in Arabic stories, with Lilith. In the Arabic legend, and among others also in *Thousand and One Nights*, we find the detail that Balqis' grave has been found in Tadmor. Seymour, referring to another source, mentions that Balqis died in Tadmor. But Tadmor is also the place of Lilith! And in the later Jewish legend, especially in the Sohar, the Queen of Sheba is identified with Lilith.

There is still another rather dark kinship of the Queen of Sheba to be mentioned, namely, the legendary Assyrian Queen Semiramis. As with Semiramis, the Arabic legend also talks of Balqis as a war heroine and the builder of miraculous buildings. [68] There must have been a lively connection between the two legendary complexes. This can be seen in the fact that still today in Assyria a lime hill, on which rest the ruins of a temple, bears the name *Tel Balqis,* hill of Balqis. It is also said in this later legend that Nebukadnezar was the son of the Queen of Sheba and Solomon, and that his wife was Semiramis. [69] As mentioned previously, Semiramis is a dark kinship. She is the lover-killing Queen, behind whom the goddess Ishtar emerges, although it is not told of her that she first asked riddles of her lovers, as it is told of the Chinese Princess Turandot

113

in *The Arabian Nights.* This motif appears, however, with Balqis herself, and so Balqis' kinship with Semiramis makes her dark background of demonic Sphinx-like femininity still more visible.

As a last parallel in their stories, the partly non-human origin has to be mentioned. It is told of Semiramis that she was the daughter of a handsome Syrian and the water goddess Derketo. For Balqis we have examples of more than one story telling about her non-human origin on one side. Now, as to the origin of the non-human stigma of the Queen of Sheba, the Arabic version of the *Kebra Nagast,* which contains some additional legends to those of the Ethiopian version,[70]says that from the earliest times, the kingdom of Abyssinia was ruled by royal princesses (this aspect of the Queen of Sheba legend will occupy us more with the Ethiopian version, where it is of main significance). So the mother of the Queen of Sheba was also a ruling queen:

> And when the mother of this Queen (i.e., of the Queen of
> Sheba) was with child of her she saw a fat and handsome
> looking goat, and she looked upon him with greedy desire,
> and said, 'How handsome the beast is! And how handsome
> its feet are!' And she longed for it after the manner of wo-
> men who are with child. And when the aforementioned
> daughter was fashioned completely in the womb of her
> mother, she had one foot like the foot of a man and an-
> other like the foot of a goat. ...And when the mother of
> the Queen had brought forth this extraordinary being,
> and had reared her, and the maiden was ready for marriage,
> she (i.e., the maiden) did not want to marry any man be-
> cause of her malformed foot; and she continued in her vir-
> ginity, until she began to reign.

This strange fascination of the Queen of Sheba's mother for an animal which has many demonic relations, from the śeʿîrîm of the Bible to the goat feet of the Devil, leads over to another group of legends, in which

114

the demonic origin of the Queen of Sheba's animal foot becomes still clearer. In a legend of northern Abyssinia the following story is told:

> The Mother of Menyelek was a Tigrê girl called Eteyê Azêb (i.e., "Queen of the South") and her people worshipped a dragon or serpent, to which each man in turn had to present as an offering his eldest daughter, and large quantities of sweet beer and milk. When the turn of her parents came they tied her to a tree where the dragon used to come for his food, and soon after this seven saints came and seated themselves under the tree for the sake of the shade it gave. As they sat a tear dropped from the maiden above them, and when they looked up and saw her bound to the tree they asked her if she was a human being and, in answer to a further question, she told them that she was bound to the tree so that she might become food for the dragon. When the seven saints saw the dragon... they killed him by smiting him with a cross. As they were killing him some blood spurted out from him and fell on the heel of Eteyê Azêb, and from that moment her heel became like the heel of an ass. The saints untied her fetters and sent her to her village, but the people drove her away, thinking that she had escaped from the dragon, and she climbed up into a tree and passed the night there. On the following day she fetched some people from the village and showed them the dead dragon, and they straightaway made her their chieftainess, and she chose for her chief officer a maiden like herself. [71]

In what follows she goes of her own accord to King Solomon, of whose medical skill she has heard, to have her deformed heel restored to its original shape; but this continuation will concern us later. Here we are mainly interested in her demonic origin. As we have seen in this legend, the Queen of Sheba escapes being a sacrificial victim of the dragon, which is worshipped by her tribe; but, remaining alive, she is

115

at least marked with a demonic sign, symbolizing her state of "belonging" to the dragon. Demonic origin, and masculinity, indicated by her being bestowed with the masculine role of a chieftain, appear here in direct connection.

Another variation of this motif is especially interesting. It combines the motif of the dragon or serpent with that of the mother of the Queen being *the direct origin* of the Queen's demoniacal stigma: In this story her mother is herself a Djinn, i.e., a demon. Tabari tells it and Hammer-Purgstall, in his famous collection of Arabic legends, retells it. [72] Here is the story:

> An emperor of China whilst hunting in the woods, had rescued a white serpent from the attack of a black serpent, and took her home. The next morning a beautiful woman stood in his room and revealed herself as a Peri (a feminine demon). Out of gratitude she promised the emperor her sister as a wife, and said that he would be happy with her if he never would ask her why she did this or that. The emperor agreed and the wedding took place. The Peri, his wife, was so beautiful that it seemed to him to be impossible to separate from her even for an instant. When she gave birth to a boy, a fire came up before the door, and the empress threw her child into it: fire and child disappeared. With the second child, a she-bear appeared. The Peri threw the little girl into her mouth and the she-bear disappeared. The emperor did not say a word, but when, in warfare in the middle of the desert, the Peri opened all the bread bags and water skins and scattered the whole supply, so that the army seemed to be exposed to starvation, he could no longer keep back, and he cornered his wife. She deplored his curiosity and said: The burnt child was not able to live, the second is still living and is nourished by the she-bear, and the food supply had been poisoned by a traitor. Soon the she-bear appeared and brought the child, but the mother disappeared. The child was Balqis, the famous Queen of Sheba. [73]

This story connects our Queen with classical anima stories, whereby it is important that her mother also shows features of superhuman, foreseeing wisdom. Here we have the same motif as in the famous Moses story in the Koran, Sura 18, and both stories also share the motif of the forbidden question: Moses goes with his servant Joshua ben Nūn in search of a fish, their food, which had escaped back into the water. They meet a man, referred to in the Koran by Allah as "one of Our servants, whom We had endowed with Our grace and wisdom." [74] Moses said to him: "Shall I follow you that you may teach me for my guidance some of the wisdom you have learnt? " But he answered: "You will not be able to endure me, for how should you have patience to bear with things you cannot comprehend? " Moses promises to be patient and not ask, and then three episodes occur as in our legend of the Peri, with the servant of Allah performing incomprehensible deeds. Moses asks him each time why he did them. "The mysterious servant of God" [75] therefore leaves him, but before doing so, he explains his deeds in the same way as our Peri, revealing his foresight and wisdom.

Jung, in his essay, "Concerning Rebirth," [76] says that these incomprehensible deeds show how ego consciousness experiences the superior guidance of fate by the Self. In our story it is the anima who possesses this higher knowledge, which human reason alone cannot understand. Just as Allah's "servant" in the Koran story is a Messianic figure representing the masculine Self, the half-human Peri in our story carries features of the feminine Self, which, however, is unredeemed and wants to be redeemed into humanness. It is dependent upon the forbidden question not being asked; if it is put, out of human impatient reasoning, the anima's redemption from the nature spell is prevented. This motif is found in many fairytales about figures who are bewitched or in some other way kept in the spell of nature, longing for redemption. I just would like to mention the mermaid, and in this connection refer to the excellent essay of Mrs. Emma Jung, "The Anima as an Elemental Being," [77] in which she gives an abundance of examples of the nature anima and the motif of her redemption, together with lucid psychological interpretations.

In our story Balqis is the daughter of such an unredeemed nature woman. In many fairy tales, the man who is not able to redeem the nature anima is drawn down into her realm, losing his humanness. Redemption is achieved, in the words of Mrs. Jung, "by recognizing and integrating these unknown elements of the soul."[78] In Tabari's legend it would have meant nothing less than that the emperor would have kept silent, and therewith accepted the most irrational actions, which could not help but hurt his masculine thinking. We can find here again the riddles of the Sphinx, but with the great difference that the anima does not want to remain in her power, does not want to destroy man, but wants him to redeem her to humanness. She wants to be recognized, accepted and changed. The recognition and acceptance can lead the man to a temporary assimilation of the realm of the anima, which can end, in unlucky cases, in his disappearing for good into the unconscious; but in prospective examples it leads to the redemption of the nature anima. Mrs. Jung mentions the example of a swan maiden (*Schwanjungfrau*) who finally became human because her human husband lived up to her condition: he let her at least temporarily go back to the water and even became a swan himself. Mrs. Jung says: "...he attempts to meet her in her own element, her *niveau*, in order to make her permanently his — conduct which should also prove of value psychologically, in relating to the anima."[79]

King Solomon in our story is also able to meet the Queen of Sheba as his nature anima by being himself close to nature (remember his understanding of the language of the animals and his magic power in the legends); and his redeeming quality lies in his presence on the throne on which Yahweh has placed him ("...and he shall be my son, and I will be his father..."),[80] this being the incorporation of a new religious development. The conversion of the Queen of Sheba, in the Arabic sources to Islam and in the Ethiopian version to the Jewish religion, expresses the redemption of the nature anima *by a spiritual development*. We will see other, more symbolic, expressions of this inner change shortly.

But after this long amplificatory journey which gave us glimpses of what oriental fantasy has to tell about the Queen of Sheba's demonic background and origin, let us come back to our legend of the Second Targum to the Book of Esther. We had left the Queen of Sheba in an embarrassing situation. She was standing on a glass floor put in by a ruse of King Solomon. On the assumption of having to walk through water, she lifted her garments, and so revealed her hairy legs. With the revelation of this demonic stigma, the process of change begins. The reflecting quality of the glass floor had trapped the Queen into involuntarily giving away her secret, which freed the way to dealing with it. It is made fully conscious when Solomon, obviously somewhat sobered, makes the dry statement: "Your beauty is the beauty of a woman, but your hair is masculine. Hair is an embellishment for a man, but it deforms a woman." It is the quality of displaced, or unredeemed, masculinity in the Queen which is stressed here by Solomon. But he does not stop with this hard statement. He commanded the Djinns to produce a depilatory called Nurah (a mixture of arsenic and quicklime); and, the legend says, this was the first use of Nurah. [81]

Now, this element of unredeemed masculinity in woman is especially in the foreground in the Abyssinian legends, where it appears, in addition to the animal stigma described in the different stories of her origin, in the masculine character of the Queen. She appears namely as an Amazon-like virgin queen who, in the course of the story, is redeemed to her femininity in its aspect of feminine relatedness to man, and at the same time "converts" to a higher spirituality. The whole inner movement and activity in these legends originates in the feminine side. They show the inner drama, as pointed out already, from the other end, not so much as a development of the anima, but as a *develop-*

119

ment of the woman who submits to a higher animus form. Naturally, also, these stories can be looked at and understood from the aspect of man's anima development. The virgin queen who does not give herself is an aspect of the anima which is not related to the masculine ego consciousness. She represents an aspect of masculinity trapped in the unconscious. A man with an Amazon anima is not ready to give feeling. Only when he is sure of his masculinity can a man give himself really with his feeling. The Amazon anima, therefore, has to be overcome and redeemed to her femininity before the *coniunctio*, the union of masculine and feminine qualities in man, can take place.

But let us come back to the Queen of Sheba as an aspect of the development of woman. The sources which I now want mainly to deal with are the Arabic and the Ethiopian versions of the *Kebra Nagast*, the *Book of the Glory of the Kings*. One legend I have already mentioned in connection with the birth story of the Queen of Sheba is the Arabic version of the Ethiopian legend; the other is the *Kebra Nagast* itself. In both of them (they are basically very similar), the Queen of Sheba is not fetched by King Solomon, but goes to him of her own accord. In the former legend she wants him to heal her goat foot, and in the latter, as we saw, she has heard of his wisdom and, longing for it, decides to visit him. The *Kebra Nagast*, especially, puts the Queen and her approach to, and experience of, King Solomon and his wisdom in the center, which, in itself, suggests looking at these versions of the story mainly from the aspect of feminine psychology and development. As I pointed out, though, it is always a matter of corresponding processes.

Let us look now at both stories, one after the other: The first is the already mentioned story from the tradition of Axum in North Abyssinia, in which the Queen of Sheba acquired her ass foot as the result of a drop of dragon blood which fell on her heel. [82] You remember that as a sacrifice for the dragon, she was bound to a tree, then was rescued by the seven saints resting under the tree who killed the dragon, untied her fetters and sent her to her village. The people, thinking she had escaped

the dragon, drove her away. Only the next day when she showed them
the dead dragon did they not only accept her coming back, but made her
their chief. This seems astonishing at first glance, but no longer so if you
look at it psychologically. Having been taken out, chosen, as the sacrifice for the dragon god, she was taboo, i.e., chosen for a ritual purpose
connected with the fate of the tribe. Such a person could not possibly
regress to a banal, normal life. She belonged to the dragon and was sacrificed to be incorporated by the tribe's demon, perhaps its totem. She
could, as it were, change her fate only by living it in another, equally
impersonal, form linked up with the life of the tribe. Instead of the
feminine and passive victim, she became the masculine and active leader
of the tribe. The story intimates that the people, seeing the dead dragon,
assumed she was the one who had killed it. Through having stimulated
the "animus court" of the seven saints by her tears, indirectly she perhaps did kill the dragon. Then she became chief and, as you remember,
chose for her first officer a *maiden like herself*. But the stigma of her
ass foot remained as a sign of her dragon background.

This is also an excellent symbol for a certain type of modern Amazon
in whom the animus is not linked with feminine feeling, but is, at it were,
an autonomous man, while the femininity remains on a level of animal
nature. Psychological virginity then becomes a means of protection
against womanhood, against being "recognized" as a woman. (Think of
the biblical term "to know" in the meaning of love-embrace.) [83] This
negative virginity can, in the modern woman, be kept up side by side
with innumerable sexual affairs, which are, in the worst cases of inner
split, nothing other than the autonomous life of the "ass foot." But in
other cases, these women consciously or unconsciously long to be redeemed to their womanhood, so that, incapable first of feminine submission, they create occasions that force them into the longed-for submission, therefore leaving it to the man to break down the wall they
have put up against the personal, the erotic, realm; thus, sometimes
the man will have to use a ruse to overcome the "man" in the woman

in order to meet the woman on her own unconscious grounds.

This is exactly what happens in our story. Soon after she became the chief of her tribe, Eteyê Azêb (as the Queen of Sheba is called in this story) heard a report of the medical skill of King Solomon. She determined to go to him so that he might restore her deformed heel to its original shape. She and her first officer dressed their hair after the manner of men, and, girding themselves with swords, they departed to the court of Solomon at Jerusalem. In this version, the Queen of Sheba comes literally as *a man* to King Solomon, which, humorously enough, is noted in the text: "Her arrival was announced to Solomon, who ordered his servants to bring the *King* of Abyssinia into his presence..." [84]

Then as soon as the Queen's deformed foot touches the threshold, it miraculously recovers its natural form. In this version it is the *genius loci* which brings about the longed-for change, i.e., heals the demonic animal stigma.[85] Had that been the only purpose for her coming, as she thought it was, she could have turned back and gone home. But becoming a woman reveals itself to be the underlying unconscious goal, of which the redemption of the animal stigma is only one part. Since this goal, however, is unconscious to her (for consciously she hid behind her masculine disguise), the wise King meets her unconscious desire on the level of her own nature by using a ruse. Being the wise king, Solomon, of course, quickly realized they were women and planned to trap them in their own feminine nature:

> When night fell he caused two beds to be made for his
> guests in his own bedroom, and he hung up in the room
> a skin with honey in it, and he pierced the skin and the
> honey dropped down into a bowl set there to catch it,
> and Solomon and his guests betook themselves to their
> beds. At night the king was accustomed to keep vigil
> with his eyes closed and to sleep with them half-open,
> and thus when the two women, who were longing to
> get off their beds and to go drink honey from the bowl,

saw him with his eyes half-open, they thought that the
king was awake, and they curbed their desire for the honey
and lay still. After a time the king woke up and closed his
eyes, but the women, thinking he was asleep, rose from
their beds and went to the bowl of honey and began to eat.
By this Solomon knew that his two guests were women,
and he got up and went with them to their beds and lay
with both of them. [86]

You will soon recognize that this North Abyssinian legend is much
more primitive than the one in the *Kebra Nagast* itself, to which I now
want to turn. In this late Christian version of the story, the "Queen of
the South" is not overly masculine. She is described as "very beautiful
in face, and her stature was superb, and her understanding and intelli-
gence, which God had given her, were of such high character that she
went to Jerusalem to hear the wisdom of Solomon."[87] But interestingly enough, just as the hoopoe bird, an intuitive hunch from the unconscious, brought the knowledge of the Queen of Sheba to Solomon in
the Jewish legend, there is also a mediator functioning in our story.
Since the movement proceeds from the woman's unconscious, it is not
surprising that it is a *mercurial figure, Tâmrîn the Merchant,* who acts
as a mediator. He traded with King Solomon and traveled often from
the land of the Queen to Jerusalem for this purpose. He was deeply im-
pressed by King Solomon's wisdom, and when he returned to Ethiopia,
he told his Queen all about it, in an enticing way. "Each morning," the
text twice repeats, Tâmrîn "related to the Queen about all the wisdom
of Solomon; he recalled the things that he had seen with the King and
described them unto her." And here is the effect of this suggestive
effort: "...the Queen was struck dumb with wonder at the things that
she heard from the merchant her servant, and she thought in her heart
that she would go to him; and she wept by reason of the greatness of
her pleasure in those things that Tâmrîn had told her...And her heart
inclined to go to him, for God had made her heart incline to go and had
made her to desire it." [88]

123

Here it is no doubt a matter of a genuine spiritual need and desire, an animus problem, which becomes the Queen's fate. This finds its expression in an impressive way when she says to her people, before leaving them in order to follow her desire to visit King Solomon: "I am smitten with the love of wisdom, and I am constrained by the cords of understanding..." Here the suffering connected with an inner process of growth rings through. The whole farewell speech is an apotheosis of wisdom. And thereby a most interesting switch takes place from a feminine image of wisdom to a masculine one. First the Queen says:

> Wisdom is an exalted thing and a rich thing: I will love her like a mother, and she shall embrace me like her child. I will follow the footprints of wisdom and she shall be with me for ever...

In the following passage it seems as if the content were more impersonal:

> Let us seek her, and we shall find her; let us love her, and she will not withdraw herself from us; let us pursue her, and we shall overtake her; let us ask, and we shall receive; and let us turn our hearts to her so that we may never forget her.

But then the process of projection takes its natural way: the great content suddenly "sits" on the *wise man*, and finally specifically on King Solomon, thus reaching a quality of inner reality in the text itself. One suddenly feels the experience of the woman being grasped by the archetype of wisdom *as incorporated in a person*. Much more than for men, I think it is true for women that they can love ideas only in their manifestation in *life*. Let us listen to her words:

> The honouring of wisdom is the honouring of the *wise man*, and the loving of *wisdom* is the loving of the *wise man*. Love the wise man, and withdraw not thyself from

him, and by the *sight* of him thou shalt become wise;
hearken to the utterance of his mouth, so that thou
mayest become like him; watch the place whereon he
hath set his foot, and leave him not, so that thou mayest
receive the remainder of his wisdom. And I love him
merely on hearing concerning him and without seeing
him, and the whole story of him that hath been told me
is to me as the desire of my heart, and like water to the
thirsty man.[89]

The last sentence ("I love him merely on hearing concerning him and
without seeing him,...") very beautifully proves what was said. The
knowledge that wisdom is *lived by a real person* is necessary for the
woman, in order that it can become an experience for her.

Now in this elaborate and more differentiated story there is naturally
no problem, at this point, of an ass foot or a goat foot. The Queen
spends six months in a separate house at King Solomon's court, conver-
sing with him every day, hanging on his every word, admiring his kind
and wise behavior.

Where does nature appear in this story, which threatens to die in a
tensionless bore? Astonishingly, or perhaps not astonishingly, it comes
in a way very similar to that tension in the previous, cruder story — in a
ruse of the King to win the virgin Queen. It is important that this happens only after the spiritual fruit of their encounter has fallen from the
tree, so to speak, in the Queen of Sheba's conversion to Yahweh. She
says:

From this moment I will not worship the sun, but will
worship the Creator of the sun, the God of Israel. And
that Tabernacle of the God of Israel shall be unto me my
Lady,[90] and unto my seed after me, and unto all my
kingdom that are under my dominion. And because of
this I have found favour before thee, and before the God
of Israel my Creator, Who hath brought me unto thee

125

and hath made me to hear thy voice, and hath shown
me thy face, and hath made me to understand thy
commandment.

When, after that, the Queen wanted to go back home, the King sent
her a message inviting her to stay longer, in order to increase her acquired
wisdom by studying everyday life in his kingdom. "I will complete thy
instruction, and thou shalt learn the administration of my kingdom..."
And the Queen answers in turn:

From being a fool, I have become wise by following thy
wisdom, and from being a thing rejected by the God of
Israel, I have become a chosen woman because of this
faith which is in my heart; and henceforth I will worship no other God except Him.

She decides to stay. "And," the text goes on, "Solomon rejoiced because of this, and...the house of King Solomon was made ready (for
guests) daily. And he made it ready with very great pomp, in joy, and
in peace, in wisdom, and in tenderness, with all humility and lowliness;
and then he ordered the royal table according to the law of the kingdom."
Now, at this splendid meal King Solomon served very spicy food, "with
wise intent," the text remarks. When everybody else had left, the King
said to the Queen: "Take thou thine ease here for love's sake until day-
break." She did not decline the invitation, but said:

Swear to me by thy God, the God of Israel, that thou wilt
not take me by force. For if I, who according to the law
of men am a maiden, be seduced, I should travel on my
journey (back) in sorrow, and affliction, and tribulation.[91]

King Solomon answered: "I swear unto thee that I will not take thee
by force, but thou must swear unto me that thou wilt not take by force
anything that is in my house." The Queen laughingly swore it, saying:

126

> Being a wise man, why doest thou speak as a fool? Shall
> I steal anything, or shall I carry out of the house of the
> King that which the King hath not given to me? Do not
> imagine that I have come hither through love of riches.
> Moreover, my own kingdom is as wealthy as thine, and
> *there is nothing which I wish for that I lack. Assuredly*
> *I have only come in quest of thy wisdom.*[92]

Thus, consciously self-contained and unaware of the inner need which made her ready to stay, the Queen then experienced *absent eros*, in the substitute form of a terrible thirst, caused by the spicy meal, which made her yearn for water. That night, assuming that Solomon slept, she went and took water from his table in order to quench her thirst. This was the trap. Her stealing of the water freed Solomon from his oath. She said to him: "Be free from thy oath, only let me drink water." And, the text goes on, "he permitted her to drink water, and after she had drunk water he worked his will with her and they slept together."[93]

In the Arabic version of the *Kebra Nagast*, the Amazon character of the Queen of Sheba comes to light even more. She denies herself to the King more consciously. The text says:

> And Solomon loved women passionately, and it came to
> pass that, when her visits to him multiplied, he longed for
> her greatly and entreated her to yield herself to him. But
> she would not surrender herself to him, and she said unto
> him, 'I came to thee a maiden, a virgin; shall I go back de-
> spoiled of my virginity, and suffer disgrace in my kingdom? '
> And Solomon said unto her, 'I will only take thee to myself
> in lawful marriage — I am the King, and thou shalt be the
> Queen.' *And she answered him never a word.* 'Strike a
> covenant with me that I am only to take thee to wife of
> thine own free will — this shall be the condition between
> us: when thou shalt come to me by night as I am lying on
> the cushions of my bed, thou shalt become my wife by the
> Law of Kings.' And behold she struck this covenant with

> him *determining within herself that she would preserve her virginity from him.* And Solomon by his wisdom in-structed her for a number of days, and he did not again demand from her the surrender of her person, and the matter was good in her sight, because she thought that he had driven her out of his mind. [94]

But then follows the same ruse with the spicy food and the thirsty Queen and the happy end!

Returning again to the Ethiopian version: The fruit of the union be-tween King Solomon and the Queen of Sheba was a son, born on the Queen's way back to Ethiopia. King Solomon had given her a ring from his finger, to be sent back with their child if it should be a boy. It was a boy, and she answered him: "Why dost thou ask me about thy father? *I am thy father and thy mother*; seek not to know anymore." But he did not stop his quest, and one day she told him, and when Beina Lekhem was 21 years old, she sent him with the ring to his father. I skip the whole story about Beina Lekhem's journey to King Solomon, his stay there and return with the Tabernacle, since we are here mainly con-cerned with the *relationship* between the Queen of Sheba and King Solomon. But one thing of importance has to be mentioned in this connection: In Chapter thirty-three we read: "Now there was a law in the country of Ethiopia that (only) a woman should reign, and that she must be a virgin who had never known man, but the Queen said (unto Solomon): 'Henceforward, a man who is of thy seed shall reign, *and a woman shall nevermore reign;* only seed of thine shall reign and his seed after him from generation to generation.'"

This means nothing less than that the law of the matriarchate, the ruling of the Amazon Queen, is broken. The Amazon Queen not only abdicates, but decrees that "a woman shall *never*more reign." Seen psy-chologically, from the point of view of animus development, the union with the animus brings about a decisive change: the positive animus, differentiated from the feminine in the symbol of the son, will rule from now on, while the woman is freed from it. This confirms a frequently occurring phenomenon in modern feminine psychology. If a woman is freed from the animus possession, by uniting as a woman with the animus, instead of *being him*, i.e., by *relating with her feminine feeling to the spirit*, she becomes both more consciously masculine, by accepting and developing her masculinity, and at the same time more feminine, because the accepted animus does not sit anymore on her femininity, twisting or destroying it.

After this discourse on the feminine aspect of the *coniunctio* between the Queen of Sheba and King Solomon, let us turn again to the masculine aspect which stands in the foreground in our legends. The half-animal, half-human anima, gifted with the cruel power of the Sphinx, is redeemed both by the solution of her riddles, i.e., by knowledge of her mystery, and by the redemption of her animal stigma.

Before going into the riddles, I would like to mention a very interesting further development which the motif of the animal foot of the Queen of Sheba has gone through in the Christian Middle Ages. That the Queen of Sheba should appear at all with this stigma in the Christian legends is significant, since in the main trend of Christian tradition, the Queen of Sheba became more and more the mystical bride. *She was identified with Shulamith of the Song of Songs*, and for the Church fathers she became (on the basis of Matthew 12:42, where it is said of the "Queen of the South" that she came from the corners of the earth to hear the wisdom of Solomon) a symbol of the pagan peoples who expect the coming of the Messiah. Thus the Queen of Sheba and King Solomon appear also with Honorius of Autun among the *Paranymphi Sponsi et Sponsae* (bridespeople of the Bride and Groom).

In the above mentioned trend of Christian tradition concerning the Queen of Sheba, her legend is linked with that of the wood of the cross, whose touch miraculously heals her animal foot. The oldest form of this legend is probably that found in the Orient, in the previously mentioned

129

Arabic version of the *Kebra Nagast*, according to which the wood of the cross came from Paradise. It came through Solomon's wisdom down to earth, carried by the fabulous giant bird *Rukh*, and it was used by Solomon in the building of the temple, because of its power to split rocks. This paradisiac wood was touched by the Queen of Sheba when she walked through the water (rather than upon the crystal floor in the Jewish legend) to the King. This wood later became the wood of the cross, and thus connects Adam with Christ; i.e., it can be looked upon as a symbol of human development from the paradisiac state of nature to the humanized or incarnated divine consciousness. But it is this development of consciousness which humanizes the anima; i.e., if the link with nature is not broken, if the *coniunctio* between nature and spirit takes place, then the result is the same whether the impetus comes from the masculine side, as in the Jewish legend, or the feminine, as in the Ethiopian. In our day, because of the obvious shadow side of patriarchal thinking, there is a tendency to depreciate patriarchy and idealize matriarchy. But it should not be forgotten that the shadow side of matriarchal origins is chaos, an undifferentiated swamp which yearns for redemption, an eternal cycle of recurring death and birth, out of which no development would have come without the new principle of Spirit breaking through. The desirable goal, as it appears in myths and legends such as ours, as well as in dreams, is not a "motherworld" in contrast to the "fatherworld," but the *coniunctio* of feminine and masculine.

This legend involving the Queen of Sheba with the wood of the cross appears also in Western Christian legends of the Middle Ages. There the Queen of Sheba is placed within a genealogical line which begins with Noah and ends with the "Magi" worshipping the Christ child. This has to do with the fact that the Queen of Sheba had been identified quite early with Sibyl, the ancestress of all magicians. With a Byzantine Chronicler of the ninth century, the monk Georgios, we find the remark that the Queen of Sheba is called Sibyl by the Greeks. Georgios thinks of the

130

Sibyl Sabbē of whom Pausanias reports, in his commentary about the prophecying woman, that she lived with the Hebrews above Palestine in the Syriac mountain hills. Alian calls her the Jewish Sibyl. [95]

Also because of the nimbus the mysterious land of Saba had as a land of magic, it lent itself easily to this identification of Sibyl with the Queen of Sheba. In the radiance of this nimbus, Bilqis, the Arabian Queen of Sheba, became in the West the magician and prophetess, and was connected as *Regina Sibylla* by the Christian legend of the West with the legend of the wood of the cross.

In the Western version, when the Queen of Sheba, i.e., Regina Sibylla, was on her way to Solomon, she came to a river, across which a plank formed the bridge. As a prophetess seeing into the future, she became aware, however, that sometime in the future the cross of Christ would be made out of this wood. Full of awe, therefore, she avoided walking over the plank. Instead she lifted her dress (you recognize again the motif of the crystal floor in Solomon's palace) and went barefoot beside the plank through the river. Then, behold, a miracle happened — for when she had traversed the river, *her web foot was changed into a human foot.* Here the redeeming quality of the wood is still more connected with the fact of the future cross. Another change is very interesting: the web foot of the elves or swan maidens in German folklore replaces the ass or goat foot of the Oriental sagas. Emma Jung, in her above mentioned essay, gives several examples of the anima as a nature being in the form of the swan maiden: among others, the Indian saga of Purûravas and Urvasî in the Rig-Veda, the Irish Saga of the "Dream of Oenghus," and the Wolunds song in the Edda, which is introduced with the motif of the swan maiden. This form of the anima is one of the oldest and occurs all over the world. The swan motif indicates psychologically the original closeness of the anima with water, the unconscious, into which she is always ready to disappear and into which, in some stories, she does indeed disappear, because her human husband is unable to allow her necessary return, from time to time, to her original

131

element. [96]   In another respect, the swan symbolizes the anima, which is difficult to grasp and hold, since it can also fly and disappear in the air. In the story of the Rig-Veda, because her husband had not lived up to the condition, the nymph Urvasî disappears forever: "I have passed away like the first of the dawns...I am like the wind, difficult to catch..." [97]

The river in our legend, replacing the crystal floor, stresses still more the transition from one shore to the other, from the nature world to the spiritual world. This motif, mirroring nothing less than an epochal happening in the development of human consciousness, must have made a correspondingly deep impression on the unconscious of the centuries, since it has frequently been painted. In most of the pictures Solomon waits for the Queen of Sheba at the other side of the river. [98]   I might mention just two examples, which seem to me to indicate the whole range of development of this legendary motif: the first is a most delightful picture in a Persian manuscript, [99] giving the full flavor of the rich imagination of the Islamic legends. It shows King Solomon sitting on his throne, his head haloed by the flame of prophecy. The Queen of Sheba approaches him, walking over the water covered with crystal leaves, revealing her hairy legs. Both royalties are surrounded with animals and Djinns, which obey their commands, and with heavenly birds, whose language is understood by Solomon. The second example is the famous, and to my feeling most sublime and moving, picture of the meeting of King Solomon and the Queen of Sheba, by Piero della Francesca, part of his frescos at Arezzo. [100]

While the connection with the animal nature of the Queen of Sheba has to be redeemed, as we have seen, in the Western legend, the other sign of her demonic background, namely the Sphinx question, disappears entirely. In the Ethiopian version, however, the animal foot is not in the picture, but the questioning of the Queen is very much in the foreground, although with quite a different emphasis. Her questions are no longer the cruelly probing ones of the Sphinx; they are not only a means of power in the hands of the Sphinx, who knows the

answer, *but are changed into the real questions of the Queen* who wants
to know, in her longing for wisdom. In our original Jewish legend, which
proves to be the fullest one concerning all the motifs — there is no doubt
that it is one of the sources for the priest Isaac, the assumed composer or
compiler of the *Kebra Nagast* [101] — one finds both elements, the redemption of the animal stigma as well as the answering of the questions. Through
the reflection of the Queen's ass foot in the mirror of the water or crystal,
a consciousness of the problem is reached which, however, is not yet its
solution; for the Queen puts her questions, which appear in the Jewish and
Arabic legends in manifold variations. Although the threatening Sphinx
atmosphere is no longer overt in these legends, it happens that in *all* variations *the putting of the questions immediately follows the revealing of
the demonic foot: so they obviously belong together.* It is the Queen
with the animal foot who puts the questions, and her redemption occurs
also in a double way — both through the alchemical process of the depilatory as well as through the answering of her questions. If we look at these
questions through the aspect which now becomes visible, *of the Sphinx in
need of and looking for redemption*, we can see that the riddles she puts
to Solomon confirm this aspect and make it still clearer.

There are three main sources for the riddles, which partly overlap:
1) The Second Targum to Esther, i.e., our basic legend; 2) Midrash
Mishle Rabba, i.e., the Great Midrash to Proverbs; and 3) Midrash
Hachephez, a Yemenite manuscript in the British Museum, which was
printed and translated for the first time in *Folklore.* [102] The first mentioned source contains three riddles; the second, four; and this recently
edited one has nineteen of them, those of Midrash Mishle, as well as a
number of other riddles, most of which are found scattered through
the Talmud and the Midrash. [103] Since I cannot go into all of them
and have to make a choice, I would like to go into the first three questions in Midrash Mishle Rabba, the Midrash to Proverbs, which some
Arabic authors have also picked up. The first one is:

> Seven there are that issue and nine that enter:
> two yield the draught, and one drinks.

Solomon answers that these are the seven days of Nidah: i.e., menstruation; nine are the months of pregnancy; two are the breasts that yield the draught; and one is the child that drinks it.[104] The second riddle the Queen puts to Solomon is this:

> A woman said to her son, thy father is my father, and
> thy grandfather my husband; thou art my son, and I
> am thy sister.

Whereupon Solomon answers: "The mother who said this to her son is one of Lot's daughters."

The third riddle, which occurs in almost all legends, is not put into words, but into action and consists of the following: The Queen sends to Solomon five hundred young men dressed like women and an equal number of young women dressed like men. (In other versions, they are 6000 each, and they are simply dressed the same way.) Solomon then has to find out which are the men and which the women. He solves the riddle by having offered to them, according to the most common version, water to wash themselves, and from the way they do it (the men use only one hand, the women both), he tells them apart. In another version he has nuts and roasted ears of corn brought to them. The males, who were not troubled with bashfulness (as the text says[105]), seized them with bare hands, the females took them by putting forth their gloved hands from beneath their garments. In still another version, the boys just spread their garments to receive their gifts while the girls bashfully used their scarves. The third riddle also has a significant background which fits well in our connection: According to Diodor, Semiramis invented the Median-Persian costume or dress of a sort which did not allow one to recognize whether the person wearing it was a man or a woman.[106] According to Ta'alabi, Baidawi and Husein, the young people are not dressed the same way, but the boys were feminine, the girls masculine dresses. Also this exchange of dress hints at cults in the service of androgynous deities, to which also Semiramis belongs.[107] Semiramis, as we know, is closely connected with Ishtar.

If we look a little closer at these riddles, we can recognize in the first one a certain similarity to the classical Sphinx riddle, inasmuch as it has also to do *with a natural law of human life*. But here it is outspokenly the natural law of *feminine* life, from the point of view of an experience of the mystery of feminine nature.

The second question points to father-daughter incest. As H. Y. Kluger showed in his article on the Book of Ruth,[108] the people of Moab, whose common ancestor originated from the union of Lot with one of his daughters, has in the Old Testament a naturelike, feminine, matriarchal significance. The incest itself occurs in a cave (whose feminine symbolism is obvious) with Lot having been made drunk, i.e., unconscious. The masculine is still entirely under the domination of the feminine, just as in the parallel myth of the birth of Adonis, child of Myrrha, the daughter of King Kinyras of Cyprus, who made her father drunk and slept with him.

Psychologically one could seen an inner sequence in the first two riddles, which seem at first glance to have no connection: the first represents *the self-enclosed nature of feminine life*; the second, *the birth of the masculine out of the father-daughter incest*, whereby the main emphasis in the Lot story rests upon the birth of the son for the woman. Consequently, this would lead on to the third riddle, whose subject is the *discrimination between masculine and feminine as specific values*. These riddles should be reflected upon by the wise King Solomon. His thinking is now the reflecting mirror, which previously was symbolized in the crystal floor. By means of this reflection, the Queen of Sheba is recognized both in her feminine mystery and also in her development as she strives toward the spirit. Thereby she could become conscious of herself, which seems to make the act of redemption complete; for it is after this that, in some legends, the union of the royal couple takes place. In this connection, it might be of value to mention also the fourth riddle in the Midrash Mishle, which anachronistically anticipates the conversion of the Queen, as a result of her inner change. It is again an enacted riddle: She brought to the King a number of persons, some circumcised and others uncircumcised, and asked him to distinguish between them. He instantly made a sign to the high priest, who opened the ark of the covenant, whereupon those that were circumcised bowed their bodies to half their height, while their countenances were filled with the radiance of the Shechinah;[109] the uncircumcised fell prone upon their faces. That means that they were unaccustomed to the holiness of the divine presence and overwhelmed by it. Here the pagan anima puts her own problem before the King, who redeems her by realizing it.[110]

There exists still another line of tradition. This line identifies the Queen of Sheba, without all the aforementioned demonic implications, with *Sophia*. I would like to mention it at least briefly. Marie-Louise von Franz gives the following information in her *Aurora Consurgens*[111]: In the alchemistic tradition the *regina austri*, the "Queen of the South" of Matthew 12:42, is Sapientia herself and she is considered like Solomon to be the author of alchemical works. She also was identified with Maria the Jewess, the "sister of Moses." According to Ruska, she appears also with the name Bilqis, as Queen of Egypt, though, and among others, she was supposed to have written a book with the beginning: "After I had climbed up the mountain..." In the patristic literature she appears also entirely on the light side, as a prefiguration of Mary. And in the hermeneutics of the Church fathers, the *regina austri* appears also as an image of the Church, as the *"regina"* or *"concubina"* of Christ, who himself is called *rex austri*. The allusion identifies this feminine figure with God himself, "who shall go with whirlwinds of the south."[112] But the south wind is, as Prof. Jung mentions in *Psychology and Alchemy*,[113] a symbol of the Holy Ghost, presumably on account of its hot and dry quality. The Holy Ghost is fiery and causes exaltation. From this context it becomes clear that the *regina austri* is, as Sapientia, a feminine *pneuma*.

In contrast to this development, in the Kabbala, as previously mentioned, the Queen of Sheba is exclusively identified with Lilith. For her

Sophia aspect we have to look to the Shechinah, the feminine inhabitation of God in man. The Queen of Sheba is, as it were, the dark sister of the Shechinah, her shadow. This discrimination indicates a split, but at the same time a differentiation, for there are very interesting relations between them in the Sohar — for instance, that God is with Lilith when the Shechinah is in exile, which would mean psychologically that when his feminine feeling is not present, he falls into his demonic destructive anima. This whole situation hints towards a further development in the divine drama and therewith in the human soul. The redemption of Lilith is yet ahead. We have a similar split between the all-light figure of Mary and the host of Lamias in folklore. The great difference is, however, that Lilith, the child-killing Lamia par excellence is here in some relationship to God, just as Satan is, [114] which is a presupposition of an integration of the dark.

In alchemy, however, we already have the experience of a union of the opposites. The image of the *coniunctio* between the Queen of Sheba and King Solomon, and its connection with the redemption of the dark Queen, found there its most complete expression, because it still embraces darkness and light, as is to be seen in some alchemistic statements mentioned in Jung's *Mysterium Coniunctionis.* [115] With the alchemists, the relationship of King Solomon to the Queen of Sheba became, as Jung points out, a pattern of spiritual love. The Queen of Sheba is the Virgin Earth, the feminine Mercury, and as Queen, the heaven in which the sun shines; She is the medium which surrounds the Sol, the natural vessel of Sol. Reading this, one is reminded of the sun worshipper Bilqis in the Second Targum to the Book of Esther. [116] In alchemy the Queen had been redeemed out of the dark; this comes through in a very deep passage in the *Tractatum Aureus de Lapide.* [117] The Queen at her apotheosis holds a discourse in which she says:

> *After death is life restored to me.* [118] To me, poor as I am, were entrusted the treasures of the wise and mighty. Therefore I, too, can make the poor rich, give grace to the humble, and restore health to the sick.

The factor of redemption is also visible in another text mentioned by Jung. Johannes Grasseus says of the white dove which is hidden in the lead and must be extracted from it: "This is that chaste, wise and rich Queen of Sheba, veiled in white, who was willing to give herself to none but King Solomon. No human heart can sufficiently investigate all this.[119]

I would like to close with Jung's truly illuminating comment on these statements. He says that, especially in the first quoted passage, we really have an identification of the Queen with Christ. From this we can see, "...how very much the queen and the king are one. As a matter of fact, the queen corresponds to the soul (anima) and the king to spirit, the dominant of consciousness. In view of this meaning of the queen, we can understand why the work sometimes is called *"Reginae Mysteria."*[120] This explanation, Jung says, "is true only of the male artifex. The situation is reversed in the case of a woman."[121]

If we ask ourselves in what way the situation could be reversed, it it seems to me that the answer is implied in the statement of the *Tractatus Aureus de Lapide* in which the Queen of the South says that after death, life had been given back to her, and she was enabled to pass on the treasures of the wise which had been confided to her. For the feminine psyche this could mean the realization (in the literal sense of the word) of the received spirit which became her own.

But what Jung further says is valid for both man and woman, as seen from their mutually different situations:

> ...a conscious attitude that renounces its ego-bound intentions — not in imagination only, but in truth — and submits to the suprapersonal decrees of fate, can claim to be serving a king. This more exalted attitude raises the status of the anima from that of a temptress to a psychopomp. The transformation of the kingly substance from a lion into a king has its counterpart in the

138

transformation of the feminine element from a serpent into a queen. The coronation, apotheosis, and marriage signalize the equal status of conscious and unconscious that becomes possible at the highest level – a *coincidentia oppositorum* with redeeming effects.[122]

∞∞∞∞∞∞∞∞∞∞∞∞∞∞∞∞∞∞

NOTES

1. Wendell Phillips, "Qataban and Sheba," *Exploring Ancient Kingdoms on the Biblical Spice Routes of Arabia,* London, 1955, p. 107.

1a. See above.

2. Op. cit., p. 109.

3. Ibid., p. 107.

4. Ibid., p. 108.

5. Compare Benzinger, *Commentary to the Book of Kings*, 1899. He stresses the legendary character of the story, seeing in it a counterpart to the story in I Kings 3:16ff of "Solomon's Judgement," which also illustrates Solomon's wisdom. The meaning of the story of King Solomon's encounter with the Queen of Sheba, however, seems to me considerably deeper.

6. Appeared in 1887.

7. Loc. cit., p. 307.

8. Sir Ernest A. Wallis Budge, *A History of Ethiopia*, 1887, vol. I, p. X. (Photomechanic reprint, published by Anthropological Publications, 1970.)

9. Op. cit., p. 193.

10. J. Deramey, "La Reine de Saba," *Revue de l'Histoire des Religions*, 1894, p. 310.

11. Ibid., p. 308.

12. Ibid., p. 308.

13. Ibid., p. 308.

14. Ed. by Conti Rossini, with French translations, in *Corpus Scriptorum Orientalium*, Series Altera, tom. VIII, Paris, 1909-10. See Sir E. A. Wallis Budge, op. cit., p. 221.

15. Budge, op. cit., p. 221.

16. Op. cit., p. 199.

17. Op. cit., p. 199.

139

18. Op. cit., p. X.

19. Op. cit., p. XVI.

20. *Antiquitates,* II, 10.

21. Compare Georg Salzberger, *Die Salomosage in der semitischen Literatur,* p. 16.

22. See André Chastel, "La Légende de la Reine de Saba," in *Revue de l'Histoire des Religions,* vols. 119-20, 1939; p. 214, n. 2; E. Blochet, *Les Peintres des manuscrits orientaux de la Bibliotheque nationale,* 1914-20, p. 297, cited there, and others, especially Ditlef Nielsen, *Der sabäische Gott Ilmukah,* Mitteilungen der Vorderasiatischen Gesellschaft, 1909.

23. According to other authors, among them Gerhard Scholem (Asmodai and Lilith, Tarbiz, 19. Annual, p. 165 [Hebrew]), *Nicaulis,* as the Queen of Sheba is called with Flavius Josephus, is the origin of *Bilqis.* Through mis-writing of *b* and *n*, (ﰉ =b, ﰈ =n) and metathesis of *q* and *l*, Bilqis or Balqis originated. In view of the popularity of *Bilqis* in Arabic folklore, it seems not very likely to me, however, that her name should have originated in literature, and even less in a technical writing error.

24. According to Wendell Phillips (op. cit., p. 250 *et passim*), *Mahram Bilqis,* an-other form of the same root.

25. Ditlef Nielsen, op. cit., p. 2.

26. *Corpus Inscriptorum Semiticarum, cit. Jewish Encyclopedia,* article "Sabeans," vol. X.

27. André Chastel, op. cit., p. 221 and Ditlef Nielsen, op. cit. (Cit. Chastel, p. 221, n. 2).

28. In the Hebrew original, Chapter 5:9-14.

29. See Benzinger, loc. cit., p. 276.

30. Ginzberg, *The Legends of the Jews,* vol. VI, p. 289, n. 38.

31. Ibid.

32. Justin Martyr, *Dialogue* 34; Tertullian, *Adversus Judaeos* 7. See Ginzberg, VI, p. 289, n. 40.

33. Kisa'î, see Salzberger, op. cit., p. 41.

34. Op. cit., p. 33.

35. Compare also the article, "Riddle," in Hastings, *Religion and Ethics,* vol. X (by James A. Kelso), p. 768-69: "With the ancients...riddles touched the serious issues of life. Life and death were involved in unravelling them..."

36. Ibid., vol. X, p. 768ff.

37. See J. B. Friedreich, *Geschichte des Rätsels,* Leipzig 1860, p. 52. See also Carl Hentze, "Religiöse und mythische Hintergründe zu Turandot," in *Antaios, Zeitschrift für eine freie Welt,* vol. I, Nr. 1, p. 21, who presents the following details: Schiller got this theme from a play of Count Carlo Gozzi

(1720-1806) whose source was a fairy tale from "Thousand and One Day," a collection of stories in the Persian language, which Pétis de la Croix brought along from Ispahan. There it has the title: "The Story of Prince Kalaf and the Princess of China." Hentze (p. 40, n. 1) refers to "Tausend und ein Tag." *Orientalische Erzählungen,* translated into German by Paul Greve, Leipzig, Insel-Verlag, 1909, 4 vols., vol. I, pp. 173-300.

38. See also Carl Hentze, loc. cit., p. 33, who arrives at a similar evaluation of Schiller's drama.

39. See Emma Jung, "The Anima as an Elemental Being," translated by Hildegard Nagel, in *Animus and Anima,* Analytical Psychology Club of New York, 1957, reprint Spring Publications, 1972, p. 78. About Benoit's "L'Atlantide," see also Cornelia Brunner, *Die Anima als Schicksalsproblem des Mannes,* Zürich, 1963, p. 108-13.

40. E. L. Rochholz, *Alemannisches Kinderlied.*

41. Milchhöfer (*Mitteilungen des deutschen archäologischen Instituts,* 1879, cit. *Encyclopedia Britannica,* ed. 1911) refers to instances in both Egyptian and Greek art where a sphinx is seen seizing and standing on a man.

42. In this connection it is interesting that also the Sirens, like the Sphinx, committed suicide, when anyone failed to succumb to their singing, i.e., could stand up to their spell. See K. Kerényi, *The Heroes of the Greeks,* p. 98.

43. *The Gods of the Greeks,* p. 50.

44. In one of the vase pictures Perseus is riding the Pegasus. See Karl Kerényi, "Perseus," in *Studien zur Analytischen Psychology,* Zürich, 1955, p. 205.

45. For an elaborate interpretation of the whole Perseus myth see Erich Neumann, *The Origins and History of Consciousness,* Bollingen Series XLII, Pantheon, pp. 213-19.

46. *The Gilgamesh Epic,* Tabl. VI.

47. 2 vols., 1889, p. 1f.

48. Loc. cit., p. 1f. Also Arabic folklore has its midday demon in white garments, who is a mankiller, *el-Mezêjara.* She confronts a man when he is alone in a desert place, calls him by name, changes her appearance and, unless overcome by verses of the Quran, catches him, so that he is pierced by the spines which she has for nipples. See William H. Worrell, "The Demon of Noonday and some Related Ideas," *Journal of the American Oriental Society,* vol. 38, 1918, p. 164.

49. See below, p. 108ff.

50. See C. H. Toy, "The Queen of Sheba," *Journal of American Folklore,* vol. XX, 1907.

51. See above, p. 99.

52. See below, p. 106ff.

53. See also Chastel, loc. cit., p. 42.

54. See above, p. 94.

55. See Hans Leisegang, *Die Gnosis,* 1924, p. 156.

56. See above, pp. 101f.

57. *CW* 5, para. 459.

58. See G. Salzberger, loc. cit., p. 15. Targum means "translation" and is the name of early translations of the biblical books into Aramaic, which are, however, not strict translations, but include a lot of legendary interpretations, so called Midrashim.

59. I follow the text as given by St. John D. Seymour, *Tales of King Solomon,* Oxford, 1924, p. 137ff. Italics mine.

60. Op. cit., p. 139. Unfortunately the author does not mention the exact source, just refers to "Mohammedan writers." Emphasis mine.

61. Told by J. E. Hanauer in his book *Folklore of the Holy Land,* 2nd ed., London, 1935, p. 187ff.

62. Loc. cit., p. 192.

63. Emphasis mine.

64. St. John D. Seymour, loc. cit., p. 139.

65. Seymour, loc. cit., p. 147.

66. William Hertz, *Gesammelte Abhandlungen,* 1905, p. 426.

67. André Chastel, *Encyclopedia Islamica,* pp. 176f., says about the *śe'īrīm,* "the hairy ones" in the desert, that they are *"le côté de la vie de la nature encore insomnis et hostile a l'homme."*

68. Hertz, loc. cit., p. 426.

69. The Kabbala took this legend up with the modification that the Queen of Sheba was not Nebukadnezar's mother, but his ancestor. (Ginzberg, *Legends of the Jews,* vol. VI, p. 390, n. 21.)

70. According to E. A. Wallis Budge, *The Queen of Sheba and her only son, Menyelek,* London, 1930. The Arabic version, on the other hand, is based on a Coptic version, p. XXXIX.

71. Enno Littmann, "The Legend of the Queen of Sheba in the Tradition of Axum," 1904, cit. Budge, *The Queen of Sheba,* etc., p. LXVII.

72. 1813, vol. I, pp. 162ff.

73. I follow a recapitulation of it in L. Leistner, loc. cit., I, p. 202f.

74. It was only later that he was identified by two commentators of the Koran, al-Bukhari (d. 870) and al-Tabari (d. 923) with Khidr, an Islamic Messiah figure. See C. G. Jung, *CW* 5, para. 282.

75. Ibid., para. 283, (see above n. 39).

76. *CW* 9, i, para. 247.

77. Emma Jung, loc. cit.

78. Loc. cit., p. 58.

79. Loc. cit., p. 50f.

80. I Chronicles 22:10.

81. Grünebaum, *Neue Beiträge zur semitischen Sagenkunde,* 1893, p. 219.

82. Littmann, op. cit.

83. See mainly Genesis 4:17 and :25, as well as I Samuel 1:19. For more about this term see my essay, "The Image of Marriage between God and Israel," *Spring,* 1950, p. 77.

84. Loc. cit., p. 68.

85. We will find this miraculous change in several other versions of the legend in more elaborate form.

86. Budge, *Queen of Sheba,* LXVIIf.

87. Budge, loc. cit., p. 17.

88. Budge, loc. cit., p. 20f.

89. Budge, loc. cit., p. 22f.; italics mine.

90. The Tabernacle, identified with Mary because the Law of Yahweh is contained in it, as later Christ in Mary, plays the main role in the continuation of the Ethiopian legend. The son of the Queen of Sheba and King Solomon – *Baina lekhem,* the "Son of the wise man" – steals, by using a ruse and killing a few workmen and priests involved in the theft, the Tabernacle while he is at King Solomon's court and brings it to Ethiopia, whereby its mana and blessing leaves Israel and goes over to Ethiopia.

91. Budge, loc. cit., p. 33.

92. Italics mine.

93. Op. cit., p. 35.

94. Budge, loc. cit., p. LIII. Italics mine.

95. See Wilhelm Hertz, loc. cit., p. 437.

96. Cf. Emma Jung, loc. cit., pp. 46ff.

97. Loc. cit., p. 47.

98. See pictures in Jeanne Lucien Herr, "La Reine de Saba et le Bois de Croix," *Revue Archéologique,* 1914.

99. Bibliotheque Nationale, Paris, reprod. in Th. W. Arnold, *Painting in Islam,* Oxford, 1924, p. 108.

100. Beautifully reproduced in the SKIRA book on Piero della Francesca.

101. See Budge, *Queen of Sheba,* p. XL.

102. *Folklore: A Quarterly Review of Myth, Tradition, Institution and Custom,* London, 1890, Vol. I, p. 349ff., "The Riddles of Solomon in Rabbinic Literature," by S. Schechter.

103. See *Jewish Encyclopedia,* "Solomon."

104. See S. Schechter, loc. cit., p. 354.

105. Midrash Hachephez, Yemen MSS, S. Schechter, loc. cit., p. 354.

106. Wilhelm Hertz, loc. cit., p. 426.

107. Wilhelm Hertz, loc. cit., p. 426.

108. "Ruth, A Contribution to the Study of the Feminine Principle in the Old Testament," *Spring,* 1957.

109. See below, p. 137.

110. Compare André Chastel, "La Légende de la Reine de Saba," *Revue de l'Histoire des Religions,* 1939, p. 42: "La Reine du Midi a donc pu, très tôt, représenter le paganisme sabéen, confronté avec la religion judaique dont Salomon, batisseur du Temple, est, pour les Juifs, comme pour les Arabes, le plus brillant représentant."

111. Bollingen Series LXXVII, 1966, p. 158ff.

112. Zacharias 9:14; in the Hebrew text *sa'ārōt tēmān,* the storms of Yemen.

113. *CW* 12, para. 473.

114. See Rivkah Schärf Kluger, *Satan in the Old Testament,* Northwestern University Press, Evanston, 1967.

115. *CW* 14.

116. See above, p. 108.

117. *CW* 14, para. 534.

118. Italics mine.

119. *CW* 14, para. 533.

120. Ibid., para. 536.

121. Ibid., para. 539, n. 428.

122. Ibid., para. 540.